Corpus Troporum

See Gordon Anderson (1929—1981). In Memoriam von seinen Studenten Freunden und Kollegen, I—II, Wissenschaftliche Abhandlungen IXL, Institute of Mediaeval Music, Henryville — Ottawa — Binningen. Vol. 1 contains a bibliography, Veröffentlichungen von Gordon Athol Anderson.

Pax et Sapientia

Published with grants from the Swedish Council for Research in the Humanities and Social Sciences.

ISBN 91-22-00825-X
ISSN 0491-2764

Almqvist & Wiksell International, Stockholm
Printed in Sweden by JINAB — Akademisk Produktion AB, Stockholm 1985

△KADEMITRYCK

ACTA UNIVERSITATIS STOCKHOLMIENSIS

Studia Latina Stockholmiensia

—————————— XXVIIII ——————————

PAX ET SAPIENTIA

Studies in Text and Music of Liturgical Tropes and Sequences
In Memory of Gordon Anderson

published by Ritva Jacobsson

CORPUS TROPORUM

ALMQVIST & WIKSELL INTERNATIONAL
STOCKHOLM/SWEDEN

ABSTRACT

Pax et Sapientia is a collection of articles about tropes and other closely related liturgical poetry and music. The volume is being published in memory of the late Australian scholar, Gordon Anderson (d. 1981), who — like the authors of these articles — worked with the Corpus Troporum project.

Tropes and the Concept of Genre (Jacobsson—Treitler)
A theoretical background to the concept of genre is given first and the possibility of using this for liturgical tropes. Concrete examples are then discussed. Most important among the examples are the entire suites of tropes written for Easter Sunday from the Apt manuscripts. Among these Easter tropes occur many very different types and systems. Such variation is typical for tropes in general. The authors find that tropes have many of the same characteristics as other genres, e.g. hymns or antiphons. They can thus be wholly biblical or written in classical hexameter. A medieval understanding of trope as genre can hardly be said to exist. The enclosing frame is instead, the mass; tropes belong to this higher level of genre organisation.

Pax et Sapientia. A Thematic Study on Tropes from Different Traditions (Iversen)
Certain themes and motifs in trope composition seem to be more prominent in one particular regional tradition than in others. This study is an attempt to follow and document four such thematic lines:
1. *Pax, lux et sapientia,* abstract epithets in the Western tradition
2. *Trinitas et unitas,* the trinitarian theme in the Northwestern tradition
3. *Haec festa praecelsa,* introductions in the Aquitanian sources
4. *Salva et parce, quos redemisti cruore,* tropes as prayers in Italian repertoires.

Les Libelli de tropes et les premiers tropaires-prosaires (M. Huglo)
Huglo proceeds from the idea that certain liturgical books originally consisted of little booklets of a few pages. Each booklet was independent and created for a special occasion or for a special liturgical act. Such booklets were called *libelli,* little books. The author produces a great quantity of references to *libelli* in the literature. In some cases one can demonstrate by analysis of trope manuscripts preserved in our day that these must have their origins in such *libelli.* This is true of, for example, the manuscript Paris BN lat 1240 — thus explaining much in the peculiar organisation of this book.

Le traité de Cantus Mensurabilis du manuscrit de Bamberg (Huglo)
This short article is an edition with brief commentary of a musical treatise in a Bamberg manuscript. The text is of practical character and has been used in the performance of polyphonic song. The text is part of the material which Gordon Anderson was working with.

"Triginta denariis" — *Musik und Text in einer Motette des Roman de Fauvel über dem Tenor Victimae paschali laudes* (W. Arlt)
The author discusses a more intricate genre, created primarily for the sophisticated connoisseur, i.e. the motett *Triginta denariis. Triginta denariis* is a musical interpolation in Gervès de Bus' *Roman de Fauvel* from the manuscript Paris BN fond français 146. The song has as its theme envy, *invidia,* and is composed to Wipo's pascal sequence. The author does an in depth analysis of both text and music and gives proof of — among other things — the refined artistry of allusion.

CONTENTS

In Memoriam

Gordon Anderson (1929—1981)

Foreword

This volume is a tribute to the achievements of a rather extraordinary scholar, and at the same time a grateful souvenir of the visit of a friend — a visit that left us a rich treasury of warm, personal memories.

Gordon Anderson came to Stockholm on a sultry night in June of 1979. It was his first visit to the Northern Hemisphere, and he had already worked with the microfilm archives in Basel and Erlangen for some weeks before. It was about ten in the evening when he arrived, and he was astonished by the light in Stockholm at that hour. We could see his enthusiasm in the brilliance and warmth of his brown eyes, a facial landmark of his that we would come to know well during the coming two months of shared discovery.

He worked in the archives of the *Corpus Troporum,* he studied Swedish sources at first hand, he worked with the collection of Swedish parchment fragments in Stockholm, he lectured some to us formally and talked much with us informally about the broad range of subjects that we represented individually — muscial, liturgical, philological, literary, all animated by the love of medie-- val chant that we had in common. It was a time of celebration, on many fronts.

The main target of Gordon's studies in that time was the tradition of medieval sequences. He aimed to make a thematic index and complete concordance of sequence sources, and a critical edition of the sequences themselves. The project was characteristic for him in a number of ways. Everyone recognizes the central position of the sequence genre in medieval poetic and musical tradition. All handbooks, dictionaries, history texts, and many individual studies provide accounts of sequences that appear on the whole to be quite definitive. But no such account, however insightful it may be in individual cases, has been based on any comprehensive overview of the repertories of sequences or their transmission.

There is a growing awareness among students of medieval poetry and music that the core of the understanding of any such tradition must be an understanding of its transmission, and that must be as comprehensive as access to the sources permits. This lies in the very nature of medieval tradition, and it is entailed even in the very definition of a genre, as is suggested in one of the essays in this volume.

So this project was very much in order, and anyone in the field would have said so. But not anyone in the field would have had the initiative and the courage to undertake it — let alone the knowledge and the ability. Initiative and courage really come down to a matter of self confidence, a quality that Gordon displayed in general. He was a man at ease with himself; the French expression says it best: *Bien dans sa peau*. And he was gifted with the technical virtues and artistic wisdom that such a project requires. *Pax et sapientia* were his benchmarks.

Gordon thought, "We need to know what this project will show," and so he undertook to do it, initially by himself, then with but one associate, Nancy van Deusen. One can well imagine how such a project would be organized in countries of the Northern Hemisphere with longer musicological traditions. A team would be organized and the work divided up among its several members, probably according to the geographical regions in which the members are specialists, funds would be raised, and the work would proceed in steady, systematic fashion. But Gordon Anderson was, after all, the man who, on the grounds of a training in classics and musicology, a practical engagement with music on a wide front, not the least of which was piano jazz performance, and a love of the subject, *made himself* the first musical medievalist in Australia.

To support his research he established the first microfilm archive of primary sources in the field, and the first library of secondary sources. These remain, dedicated to his memory, as a center for continued research in medieval studies, in the vast sheep country where his University of New England lies. And then he began to train students, some of which have by now produced theses and dissertations, as well as some other publications.

By 1979 he had won for himself a position of respect as a major but mysterious figure in the field, virtually without having spoken face to face with another professional musicologist working in medieval studies, and without having held a medieval manuscript in his hands. That this is the career of an extraordinary pioneer can be read from a *curriculum vitae*. But that impression was doubly reinforced in personal contact with the man. The broad, Australian strain in his speech, the unassuming manner, and — ironically — the strong look of the body, suggested a man turning over new ground in hard places.

As in the case of the sequence project, it was typical of Gordon to identify central tasks in areas where the discipline has behaved as though things were understood, when they were really not, but where application and skill could produce understanding. This is nowhere better recognizable than in the projects on which he set his students to work. Here are two examples:

1) Every properly trained student of musicology will be able to say about tropes in relation to traditional chants that they involve the alternation of phrases of the traditional chants with trope verses. But very few students will have had the experience of actually trying to link a set of trope verses to the phrases of a chant in performance; and the same can be said of their teachers. Gordon set a doctoral student to trying to do just that for an entire gradual of

the 11th century, using the tropes provided in a separate section of the same book. No one had ever done that before; i.e.no one had ever gone through the process of doing what singers of the time are thought to have done, in order to learn how it worked. What is characteristic for Gordon is posing the question, what was it really like, and what can we learn from the effort to find out? In this case a great deal has been learned about questions that no one had even thought to ask before.

2) The texts of *Ars antiqua* motets are poetic. The parameters of their form are syllable-count, accentual pattern, and rhyme-scheme, and it is on the basis of these factors that the texts have been edited. But the editions entail many arbitrary decisions and inconsistencies about the layout of the texts, in terms of the articulation of verses. That is, accentual pattern, syllable count, and rhyme scheme alone do not provide sufficient information regarding the intended formal articulation of the poetry. But medieval composers were close readers of the poetry that they set. The articulation of phrases in medieval music corresponds to the composers' reading of the poetry in terms of its constituent word groupings and associations. A medieval melody is evidence of the structure of its text, as that was read by the composer. No one had ever tried to read motet texts on that evidence, and Gordon set one of his doctoral students to doing so with the Montpellier motet codex. The result is a new edition of the texts on consistent criteria as regards formal layout, and with the authority of a contemporary reader's interpretations behind it.

Gordon's engagement with medieval music in his own work may be described in terms of concentric layers. The core was the preparation of an edition, which became the occasion for an open encounter with the particular problems of editing that material — problems of notation, rhythm, text layout, etc. Such problems were addressed head-on and systematically, often in separate studies. Some of his most important contributions were studies of that sort. And finally there were critical studies, which reflected an engagement beyond the technical, editorial problems. Over all, it was the practice of Philology, in the broad, humanistic sense of that term.

This book is dedicated in affection and admiration to the memory of Gordon Anderson, man and scholar.

Leo Treitler

Gunilla Björkvall
Gunilla Iversen
Ritva Jacobsson

Michel Huglo

Les « Libelli » de Tropes et les premiers Tropaires-Prosaires

La typologie du *libellus* liturgique a été abordée pour la première fois à ma connaissance, par Niels Krogh Rasmussen dans sa thèse de 1977 sur les Pontificaux du Haut-Moyen-Age.

Cette notion très féconde sur le *libellus,* que l'on doit aux hagiographes Guy Philippart et François Dolbeau, s'est révélée de grande importance pour l'histoire de la formation des livres liturgiques que j'appellerais de seconde épopontifical, hymnaire, processionnal, tropaire-prosaire et aussi, bien entendu, en hagiographie.

Dans une lettre adressée au Père Rasmussen le 29 février 1980, le Père Gy a défini en quatre points précis les caractéristiques du *libellus* liturgique :
— 1 : le *libellus* comporte seulement un cahier ou tout au plus deux à trois quaternions ;
— 2 : à l'origine, ces cahiers étaient indépendants ;
— 3 : le *libellus* n'est pas relié ;
— 4 : au point de vue liturgique, le *libellus* a pour objet non pas l'ensemble des fonctions d'un ministre — par exemple l'évêque — ou l'ensemble de l'année liturgique, mais seulement une fête déterminée ou une action liturgique *(Agenda)* particulière.

Avant de développer et, au besoin, de discuter ces notions, il importe d'examiner le sens exact de *libellus,* depuis l'Antiquité classique jusqu'à l'aube du Haut Moyen-Age, à l'aide du *Thesaurus linguae latinae.* Le terme y occupe une place importante (VII, 2, 1262—1270). Pour le Haut Moyen-Age, il faut naturellement consulter le formidable matériel rassemblé à l'Académie de Munich, pour la préparation du *Mittellateinisches Wörterbuch.*

Libellus a deux sens principaux : d'abord le sens d'écrit en général, puis le sens de livre.

1. En Droit romain, *libellus* concerne un rapport judiciaire ou le texte d'un jugement (*libellus divortii* dans le Digeste). Plus tard, sous l'empereur Dèce (248—251), *libellus* désigne le certificat attestant qu'un citoyen avait offert un sacrifice aux dieux païens et que, par conséquent, il ne pouvait être persécuté : c'est alors que certains chrétiens achetèrent à prix d'or un tel certificat, sans pourtant sacrifier aux dieux romains, et furent dénommés *libellatici. Libellus* peut encore concerner un billet, une lettre d'affaire ou même une longue épître, telle que, par exemple, l' *Epistola seu libellus sancti Hilarii*[1].

2. Le deuxième sens, que j'appellerais « bibliographique », est évidemment plus intéressant pour notre recherche. *Libellus* désigne soit un livre, par exemple chez Cicéron, par artifice de style pour éviter la répétition de *liber ;* soit un manuel, par exemple un manuel de grammaire, soit parfois le chapitre d'un livre, par exemple dans les *Vitae patrum.* Il n'a habituellement pas le sens diminutif de « petit livre », puisqu'on a éprouvé le besoin de créer *libellulus (Thesaurus* VII, 2, c. 1270) : notons en passant qu'au Moyen-Age, peut-être par accès de modestie, on a parfois préféré *libellus* à *liber,* même pour des ouvrages de quelque importance. Enfin, le Thesaurus a relevé dans l'Apocalypse (X, 10) deux traductions différentes de βιβλαρίδιον; la *Vetus Itala* l'a traduit par *libellum,* tandis que la Vulgate a préféré *librum.*

Finalement, c'est chez Grégoire de Tours au VIe siècle, que nous rencontrons pour la première fois le terme *libellus* appliqué à deux reprises au livre de prières à l'usage du prêtre (*Thesaurus* VII, 2, c. 1270), livre qu'à Rome on devait appeler plus tard « sacramentaire ».

Nous arrivons au Moyen-Age où la littérature latine a pris un essor considérable : les ouvrages en un livre, deux livres, trois livres sont légion. Rencontre-t-on des *libelli* dans l'intitulé des titres ? A défaut de recherche systématique, on peut glaner quelques éléments dans la littérature de l'époque carolingienne et ensuite dans les *libelli* eux-mêmes qui ont survécu dans les recueils actuels.

Les relations étroites qui unissaient Alcuin (d. 804) et Benoît d'Aniane (d. 821), le grand réformateur de la vie monastique et le savant liturgiste, sont bien connues. Ardon, le biographe de Benoît, nous rapporte que son Abbé avait pieusement conservé les lettres d'Alcuin et qu'il en avait confectionné un recueil — « *inviolabili se illi caritate conjunxit, ita ut ex suis epistolis ei saepe directis adgregatis in unum unus conficeretur libellus* »[2]. Evidemment ce *libellus,* formé de feuillets épars ne relevait pas du genre de livret que nous recherchons : mais la copie de cette collection a dû certainement former un *libellus.* De Benoît d'Aniane nous avons conservé un *libellus* liturgique qui a été analysé par Dom Wilmart[3].

A Centula, Angilbert avait organisé suivant un cérémonial quelque peu compliqué, des processions dans la grande basilique dédiée à saint Riquier : son *Institutio,* nous dit Hariulf[4], était consignée dans « *quidam libellus* ». Ailleurs, le chroniqueur désigne l'*Institutio* sous le terme de *libellus Angilberti*[5].

Le terme *libellus* est assez fréquemment employé pour désigner — notamment dans les anciens catalogues de bibliothèques médiévales — les opuscules et petits traités qui servaient habituellement à l'enseignement des arts libéraux, surtout le Quadrivium et plus particulièrement, peut-être, pour les traités de musique. Ainsi, le catalogue des livres de Hartmut en 883 mentionne « *Bedae libelli duo de natura et temporibus* »[6], tandis qu'à Fulda le catalogue du XVIe siècle oppose le *Liber Prisciani grammatici* à un *Libellus Prisciani,* distinction qui doit bien correspondre à une réalité concrête.

Dans l'enseignement de l'*Ars musica* — la théorie — et dans la pratique, le *libellus* tient une place importante. Ainsi, Aurélien de Réomé, qui incorpore un tonaire dans son traité de musique (chap. VIII—XIX), rédigé entre 840 et 849, prescrit aux chantres de relire son traité : « *hunc libellum cantoribus prae-bemus relegendum* »[7]. De ce fait, son tonaire abrégé tient tout entier sur trois quaternions.

Du traité et du tonaire de Bernon, qui fut « polycopié » à Reichenau au dé-but du XIe siècle à destination des églises et monastères du Saint-Empire il nous reste un seul exemplaire traité comme *libellus tonarius*[8] qui comprenait jadis cinq cahiers — aujourd'hui, il en manque un, l'avant-dernier — écrits par Udalricus[9], les autres copies ayant été englobées dans les collections scolaires de traités de musique.

Enfin, le remarquable traité de musique de la seconde Renaissance caroling-ienne, la *Musica enchiriadis* (ca. 860—870), éditée par le Dr. Hans Schmid[10], porte le titre de *Liber . . .* dans la plupart des manuscrits, mais avec la variante *libellus* dans quelques témoins tardifs[11]. De fait, le manuscrit de Freising (Clm 6409 = ms. F de Schmid) et celui de Cologne (ms. K) permettent de constater que la *Musica Enchiriadis,* indépendante à l'origine de la *Scolica enchiriadis* et sans le chapitre XIX (interpolé), peut tenir sur un quaternion supplémenté d'un feuillet intercalaire : le feuillet supplémentaire est souvent inséré à la fin du cahier, entre les deux derniers feuillets quand le scribe s'aperçoit que seize pages ne suffiront pas pour copier son texte.

Lorsque, vers la même époque, Notker le Bègue rédigea à Saint-Gall ses pre-miers essais de séquences, il se servit pour écrire, nous dit-il dans son *Proe-mium,* de rouleaux *(rotulas)* ; ses vers furent ensuite reportés sur un *libellus,* puis en 884, sur un *codicellus* destiné à Liutward de Vercelli, mais dont les ini-tiales étaient sûrement plus soignées que celles du *libellus* de l'étape intermé-diaire.

Ultérieurement, c'est à dire vers 950, les compositions de Notker identifiées en 1947 par W. von den Steinen, grâce à la critique interne, ont été englobées dans un *corpus* liturgique de séquences qui fut rapidement diffusé dans les pays de langue germanique.

Cet exemple est intéressant pour notre enquête, car il illustre assez bien la succession des étapes qui séparent la période de composition de la période de grande diffusion. Au même instant, nous découvrons l'énorme hiatus chrono-logique qui sépare les témoins subsistants actuellement des tous premiers re-cueils de proses ou de tropes : les premiers prosaires, les premiers tropaires.

De ces considérations préliminaires découlent naturellement la première proposition, qui donne la caractéristique formelle du libellus :

1. « *Le libellus comporte seulement un cahier ou tout au plus deux ou trois quaternions* ».

a. Un cahier : ce peut être parfois un ternion. Ainsi par exemple, pour le libel-lus de Sainte-Foy de Conques (dans le ms Paris, B. N. Lat 1240), qui sera analysé tout à l'heure, ou encore pour le petit *libellus*-processionnal donnant les antiennes du dimanche des Rameaux, qui appartenait autrefois au Dr. Werner Wolffheim de Berlin, et qui se trouve actuellement à la Public Library de New York[(12)].

b. Parfois, le *libellus* comprend deux ou trois cahiers : ainsi, les *quaterniones de tonis,* mentionnés dans l'ancien catalogue de Saint-Gildas-de-Berry[(13)]. Ce titre semble se rapporter à un tonaire plutôt qu'à la *Commemoratio brevis* dont l'exposé sur la psalmodie des huit tons ne pouvait suffire à remplir un seul quaternion! . . .

2. « A l'origine, ces cahiers étaient indépendants ».

C'est évident, si on n'avait pas redouté leur perte, on n'aurait pas regroupé ces petits livrets épars dans des recueils qui se présentent à nous aujourd'hui de façon disparate. Revenons au Paris, B. N. ms. lat. 1240, qui contient plusieurs *libelli* hagiographiques. Au milieu d'eux, la Passion et l'Office de sainte Foy. Ce *libellus* a été plié en deux, sans doute pour être emporté en voyage et il porte encore aujourd'hui, en milieu de page, la marque des plis, tous dans le même sens. Souvent, la première page des *libelli,* mais aussi des petits livrets autrefois indépendants, porte les traces brillantes d'une usure provenant de l'absence de reliure.

3. « Le libellus n'est pas relié ».

Tout au plus sont-ce la première et la dernière pages non écrites qui servent de couverture au *libellus.* Le cas n'est pas fréquent, mais on saisit de cette indication pourquoi certains textes, autrefois transcrits sur un ou deux quaternions, commencent encore aujourd'hui au verso du premier feuillet d'un manuscrit au lieu de débuter au recto. Tel est le cas dans quelques manuscrits de la *Musica Enchiriadis*[(14)].

A propos de reliure de manuscrits, il faut rappeler qu'autrefois on distinguait pour les livres deux types principaux de reliure. Les livres étaient habituellement reliés :

1°/*in asseribus,* c'est à dire au moyen de planchettes épaisses attachées entre elles par des « nerfs ». L'expression vient du catalogue de Cantorbéry à propos des traités de la *Musica* de Boèce. La plupart des manuscrits de Fleury ont conservé leur reliure de bois recouverte ou non de peau blanche.

Souvent, dans les écoles, les livres de consultation usuelle étaient enchaînés *(catenati)* par un anneau fixé au plat inférieur : ainsi, à Saint-Emmeran[(15)] ou à la Sorbonne dès le XIIIe siècle[(16)].

2°/*in pergameno* ; c'était, suivant un texte publié par Bernhard Bischoff[(17)], la reliure habituelle des livres universitaires d'usage privé.

Les manuscrits sans reliure sont parfois conservés *in quaternionibus*[(18)]. Ces deux ou trois quaternions restant attachés ensemble ou peut-être pas attachés du tout, d'où la nécessité de les regrouper en recueils.

4. « *Au point de vue liturgique, le libellus a pour objet non l'ensemble des fonctions d'un ministre, par exemple l'évêque, mais seulement une fête déterminée ou une action liturgique (Agenda) particulière* »,

« Une fête déterminée » : ce peut être une *fête nouvelle* qui se répand peu à peu dans toute l'Eglise — telle par exemple la Toussaint au IXe siècle ; la fête de la Sainte-Trinité au Xe siècle ou encore la Fête-Dieu au XIIIe siècle — ou une fête locale, telle que par exemple celle d'un martyr dont on reçoit les reliques — cas assez fréquent au IXe siècle — ou encore celle d'un évêque ou d'un abbé reconnus comme saints et honorés par un nouvel office propre : les exemples sont nombreux au XIe siècle.

Reprenons ces deux catégories :

1°/ Pour la diffusion de l'office propre célébrant la fête de tous les saints, on peut citer en exemple un remarquable *libellus* contenu dans un quaternion qui se trouve aujourd'hui relié dans un recueil de Fleury-sur-Loire conservé à Orléans (ms. 261) : ce *libellus* parfaitement écrit et neumé ne semble pas originaire de Fleury, mais a été modifié par grattages d'incipit pour être adapté aux usages liturgiques de Saint-Benoît-sur-Loire. Sur la dernière page restée blanche, on a ajouté à la fin du XIe siècle, un *Gloria in excelsis* tropé, composé pour la fête de tous les Saints. Voilà un exemple très intéressant qui nous explique comment, par compilation de deux *libelli* nous trouvons parfois dans les anciens antiphonaires — par exemple celui du Mont-Renaud, de la fin du Xe siècle — deux usages parallèles, mais divergents pour un même office, justement celui de la Toussaint[19].

La diffusion de l'Office composé par Etienne de Liège pour le dimanche de la Sainte Trinité, premier office qui observe la loi de succession des huit tons pour le choix des psalmodies et des timbres de répons, a dû se faire au moyen de *libelli*[20].

Pour la diffusion des offices de la Fête-Dieu, dont l'histoire est très complexe, il faut tenir compte de ces *libelli* contenant l'office et la messe de la nouvelle fête, qui ont circulé isolément ou bien qui ont été insérés dans les livres liturgiques plus anciens.

Deuxième catégorie de *libelli* : ceux qui nous transmettent les offices locaux ou offices propres. Mais ici, attention à ne pas confondre *libellus* et « recueil hagiographique ».

Le meilleur exemple en l'occurrence pour mettre en relief la distinction est celui des offices de Sainte-Foy-de-Conques en Rouergue, sur lequel je voudrais apporter ici quelques informations. En effet, les bibliothèques de France, d'Allemagne, de Suisse, d'Angleterre *etc.* contiennent tellement de petits recueils hagiographiques qu'il est nécessaire de bien s'entendre sur les termes et sur les réalités codicologiques qu'ils recouvrent.

Le culte de sainte Foy, martyre d'Agen, doit en partie son essor aux migrations, par les routes de pélerinage, qui convergeaient sur Ostabat pour amorcer le *camino francès* sur le versant méridional des Pyrénées.

Il nous reste aujourd'hui deux offices totalement différents pour célébrer sainte Foy : l'un, précédé d'une lettre d'approbation de Pascal II, reconnue aujourd'hui comme un faux, qui se trouve dans un manuscrit du XIIe siècle de Sainte-Foy-de-Sélestat[21]. C'est l'office le plus récent. L'autre office, plus ancien, est contenu dans deux manuscrits de la Bibliothèque nationale lat. 1240, du fonds de Saint-Martial et le ms. 443 des Nouvelles acquisitions latines, qui a reçu des faussaires à la solde de Libri une reliure en ais de bois, grossièrement imitée de la vieille reliure d'Orléans 347, à l'intérieur de laquelle on voit encore aujourd'hui le trou béant causé par le larcin du trop célèbre inspecteur des bibliothèques de France sous Napoléon III[22].

Pour reconstituer le manuscrit dans son intégrité, il faut rapprocher des manuscrits de Paris et d'Orléans un fragment de Leyde et un feuillet retrouvé dans le fonds de la Reine à la Vaticane par Monseigneur Victor Saxer[23].

Ce qui est fort suggestif pour notre enquête, c'est le fait que, dans les deux manuscrits parisiens — celui de Saint-Martial et celui des Nouvelles Acquisitions — nous trouvons le même office de part et d'autre, mais avec une différence importante mise en évidence sur le tableau hors-texte : dans le lat. 1240, nous avons l'office monastique à 12 antiennes et 12 répons et la messe de Sainte-Foy avec un seul alleluia[24]. Dans le manuscrit des nouvelles acquistions latines nous avons bien le même office, certes, mais aux places normales, à la fin du répons des Premières Vêpres et à la fin de chaque nocturne, un *neuma* de répons à motifs répétés (∂ = *duplicatur*) suivi d'une prose (*prosa* et non pas, ici, *prosula*). A la fin, un *Benedicamus Domino* inconnu du ms. lat. 1240.

Ce qui est fort remarquable, c'est que ce petit cahier plié en deux, à l'écriture très serrée, du lat. 1240 porte à la fin, après le nom du copiste, le titre de *libellus*. (Voir le tableau hors-texte).

Le manuscrit des nouvelles acquisitions latines est tellement plus riche en pièces, tellement plus orné d'initiales à entrelacs sur fonds de couleurs[25], tellement plus complet en récits hagiographiques en latin et en langue d'oc qu'il ne répond plus du tout à la notion de libellus, *stricto sensu*. C'est l'amplification d'un ancien *libellus* mais ce n'est plus un *libellus*.

J'ai passé en revue un certain nombre de ces offices propres qui sont très fréquents dans les recueils hagiographiques : dans la plupart des cas, ils ne forment pas une unité codicologique individuelle : ils ont été copiés et agrémentés d'initiales d'après d'anciens *libelli* tout simples, comme celui du lat. 1240. Ils ne forment plus de *libelli*.

Les offices propres suivants sont insérés dans des recueils hagiographiques de confection généralement très soignée, avec initiales peintes ou historiées : ils procèdent évidemment d'anciens *libelli,* mais ne sauraient être considérés comme tels dans leur état actuel.

PARIS B N Lat. 1240, f. 183—188
f.185 [IN I VESPERIS]
R̸/ Emissiones tuae . . . Libani, alleluia
  V Veni sponsa

[AD NOCTURNOS]
f.186 R/⁴ Gloriosa Dei Virgo Fides . . .
  V Certandum
    Gloria Patri

f.186v R/⁸ Furore succensus . . . a — vertitur.
  V Contemptis V Gloria Patri

f.187 R/¹² Jam nunc o venerabilis sponsa.
  . . . foveant nos in secula.
  V Perac — — — ta virtutum feliciter
    Gloria Patri . . .
f.188v OFFICIUM (chants de la Messe)
  Alleluia V̄ Apparuit Virgo Fides
DUPLEX BONUM EST : BERNARDUS
PRESBITER :
IUBENTE SAIONE GRAMMATICO :
HUNC : LIBELLUM :
SCIPSIPSIT (sic !) : DEO GRACIAS etc.

PARIS B N n. acq.lat. 443
f.1 IN VIGILIA SCE FIDIS AD VESP.
  R/Emissiones tuae
  V Veni sponsa
  V Gloria Patri
  Al — — ∂ — — ∂ — — (le)-lu-ja
  Prosa Candida tu quia super lilia . . . voce
ovatizant. Alleluia
f.2 ANS IN NOCT. f.4 RESPONSORIA
f.5 R/⁴ Gloriosa Dei Virgo Fides
  V̄ Certandum . . .
    Gloria Patri
f.5v Supe — — — raret
  Prosa O vere sancta prerogative . . .
f.6v R/⁸ Furore succensus . . . a — vertitur
  V̄ Contemptis V Gloria Patri
  A — ∂ — ∂ — ∂ — vertitur
Prosa: Theorica referta qui agnicia.
f.8 R/¹² Jam nunc o venerabilis
  . . . foveant nos in secula.
  V Perac — — ta virtutum feliciter
    Gloria Patri
f.8v Foveant — — ∂ — — nos in secula
  Prosa Que super titania iam rutilant . . .
. . . . .
f.14v Benedicamus altitrono domino
    qui sue martiri Fidei dedit vivere celo
    quia ignis exusta incendio
    carnis metam excessit gladio.
    Deo voce excelsa dicamus eia
    omnes una gracias regi regum qui
      gubernat secla,
    quem per albentia lilia
    sequitur sponsum Fides sanctissima
    dulce decantans carmen, alleluia.
    Alleluia (III) Apparuit Virgo Fides . . .

L. DELISLE; *Cabinet des Mss,* I,p. 390
G. BEYSSAC; *Colophons.* . . I, 1965, n°2012
(Rectifications de J. Vezin).
Catalogue général des manuscrits latins, I, Paris, B.N. 1939, p. 459.

L. DELISLE; *Catalogue des mss. des fonds Libri et Barrois,* Paris, 1898, p. 15—16.
Br. STÄBLEIN, *Schriftbild der einstimmigen Musik,* Leipzig, 1975, Abbild. 35 (= f.4).

Ainsi, l'office neumé de saint Vaast[26] ne commence pas à un début de cahier dans le ms d'Arras 734 (686), mais en milieu de cahier (f. 81v—89v). L'office de St. Wandrille a été ajouté sur les premières pages d'un des manuscrits de l'abbaye de St. Bertin (St. Omer 764, f.1 A — 3 B) : écriture, initiales, notation sont tracées de mains différentes de celles qui ont confectionné le reste du manuscrit.

L'office des deux premiers évêques de Sens, Potentien et Savinien, a été ajouté à la fin du XIIᵉ siècle sur des pages restées vides d'un manuscrit du XIᵉ siècle — comme dans le cas précédent, on a dû reporter sur un support disponible l'office composé antérieurement et écrit sur rotulus[27].

Il faudrait étendre l'enquête aux différents témoins des offices des saints Serge et Bacchus d'Angers[28], de saint Maur[29], de l'ancien office de saint Rémi[30].

Le deuxième objet du *libellus* liturgique est la transmission d'une *action liturgique* particulière ou *Agenda*. Le regard se porte directement sur les *Ordines Romani* du Haut Moyen Age : si nous possédons plusieurs collections d'Ordos romains du IXe siècle, et des copies de tel ou tel Ordo transcrit sur des feuillets vierges de textes, par ex. à Bamberg, je crois qu'il serait difficile de retrouver un Ordo romain isolé transcrit sur *libellus*[31].

Pour l'Office des morts, la situation est un peu différente : la Messe des morts n'appartient pas au Graduel grégorien primitif et l'Office des défunts ne fait pas partie de l'archétype de l'Antiphonaire grégorien. Alors, d'où viennent ces deux parties importantes de la liturgie des défunts ? C'est un problème. Pour le moment, nous constatons que l'office des Morts a circulé sous forme de *libellus* avant d'être reporté dans un recueil liturgique plus important, tel que le Rituel d'Asti du Xe siècle[32]. Ainsi, dans un *libellus* de la Trinité-de-Vendôme formé d'un seul quaternion, relié dans un recueil de la Bibliothèque nationale de Paris[33].

J'en arrive enfin aux tropaires-prosaires : dans son catalogue des tropaires-prosaires[34] H. Husmann a observé que chaque section importante des manuscrits de Saint-Martial et de Saint-Emmeran, les tropes du Kyrie, les proses, les tropes du Sanctus et de l'Agnus, démarraient à un début de cahier, souvent avec une initiale plus importante. Il découle de cette observation que les prosaires ont dû être copiés sur des *libelli* analogues à celui que Notker avait constitué en 884.

Il est également fort probable que les premiers tropaires d'introït ont été recopiés et enrichis aussi de pièces nouvelles, sur des collections du genre de Vienne 1609 contenue dans un ou deux cahiers[35]. Les *libelli* de tropes ont disparu mais leur contenu pourrait être reconstitué, grâce aux tables des éléments qui figurent dans chaque volume du *Corpus Troporum*[36]. La filiation des tropaires aquitains, qui a été tentée par plusieurs chercheurs[37], ne peut s'appliquer qu'à telle ou telle partie de ces tropaires, non à l'ensemble du livre formé par la circulation des *libelli* et par leur fusion dans des recueils liturgiques.

Ainsi, la notion de *libellus* se révèle extrêmement féconde pour la recherche dans les domaines où le Moyen Age a produit des oeuvres nouvelles : opuscules théologiques, collections canoniques[38], traités de comput[39], de mathématique et de musique[40], recueils de tropes, de séquences primitives, de séquences rythmées et rimées[41]. La réussite de l'enquête repose sur une observation codicologique rigoureuse, condition de toute recherche scientifique.

Notes

(1) MIGNE, *Patrol.lat.* c.733 — 750 : ce texte a été édité par J.C. Trombelli qui n'a pas bien précisé le dépot du manuscrit qu'il avait découvert.

(2) M.G.H. SS. XV, 210. La correspondance d' Alcuin, qui compte 232 lettres, a été éditée par E. Dümmler dans M.G.H. *Epistolae IV, Aevi karolini II* (1895), p. 18—481 et par Colin Chase, *Two Alcuin Letter-Books,* edited from B.M. Ms. Cotton Vespasian A XIV. Toronto, 1975 (Toronto Medieval Latin Texts). Malheureusement, deux épitres seulement nous restent de la correspondance entre les deux auteurs : les ép. 56 et 57. Cette dernière fait aussi allusion à la même correspondance.

(3) André Wilmart, « Un livret bénédictin composé à Gellone au commencement du IXe siècle » *Revue Mabillon,* 12 (1922), p. 119—133.

(4) Hariulf, *Chronique de St. Riquier,* éd. F. Lot (1984), XXV, 101.

(5) *ibid.* p. 70 et note *i* (le terme semble dû à l'éditeur : il ne figure pas au Glossaire final.)

(6) Paul Lehmann, *Mittelalterliche Bibliothekskataloge Deutschlands und der Schweiz,* Erster Band : Die Bistümer Konstanz und Chur, München, 1918, p. 87.

(7) *Musica disciplina,* c. XX, ed. L. Gushee, C.S.M. 21 (1975), p. 131.

(8) Vaticane, Palat. 1344, base de l'édition de Gerbert *(Scriptores . . .* II, 79—83), qui n'a pas comblé cette lacune en se servant des nombreux manuscrits à sa disposition (cf. M.Huglo, *Tonaires,* Paris, 1971, p. 266—267).

(9) Ce scribe peut-il être identifié avec l'auteur des *Consuetudines cluniacenses?* Udalric, après un séjour à Cluny à partir de 1052, avait fondé Zell en Forêt Noire.

(10) Hans Schmid, *Musica et Scolica enchiriadis, una cum aliquibus tractatulis adiunctis.* München, 1981. Bayerische Akademie der Wissenschaften. Veröffentlichungen der Musikhistorischen Kommission, Band 3.

(11) H. Schmid, p.3.

(12) New York, Public Library, Music Division (Lincoln Center), Mus. Res °MFN.

(13) Ch. Kohler, « Inventaire de la bibliothèque de St. Gildas-en-Berry » : *Bibliothèque de l' Ecole des Chartes,* 47, 1886, p.104.

(14) Munich, Bayerische Staatsbibl. Clm 6409 (Freising), Clm 14649 (St. Emmeran de Ratisbonne).

(15) Voir par ex. les traités de philosophie avoisinant la *Musica enchiriadis* (Munich, Clm 14272 et Clm 14372 : l'anneau rattachant le livre à la chaîne a été scié !).

(16) L. Delisle, *Le Cabinet des manuscrits de la Bibliothèque nationale,* Vol. 3, Paris 1881, p. 9 — 72. Dans ce catalogue rédigé en 1338, les livres d'enseignement sont suivis de la mention *cathenatus :* voir par ex. le recueil de traités de musique Paris, B.N. lat. 16662, cité dans mes *Tonaires,* p. 360.

(17) Dans ses *Mittelalterliche Studien* II, p.145, Bernard Bischoff cite le Catalogue Menger de St. Emmeran de Ratisbonne : « In pergameno secundum morem scolarium bene ligatus »

(18) G. Becker, *Catalogi bibliothecarum antiqui,* Bonn 1885, p. 111, n° 443.

(19) *Paléographie musicale,* tome XVI.

(20) P. M. Gy dans *Revue des sciences philosophiques et théologiques* 64, 1980, p. 495.

(21) Sélestat, Bibl. municipale 22 (95).

(22) L. Delisle, *Catalogue des manuscrits des fonds Libri et Barrois,* Paris, 1888, p.15—16. Remarquons que le tonaire qui suit l' office de ste. Foy vient du ms. 240 d' Orléans; cf.M.Huglo, *Les Tonaires,* Paris, 1971, p. 158—159.

(23) Vaticane, Regin. 467 : cf. Mgr. V. Saxer dans *Rivista di Storia della Chiesa in Italia,* 26 (1972), p.188.

(24) *Apparuit Virgo Fides :* ce verset d'alleluia se retrouve dans la liturgie du diocèse de Clermont (Clermont-Ferrand, Bibliothèque municipale et universitaire, Ms. 73). Faut-il expliquer ce transfert de pièce par le fait que, selon S. Swieckowski *(Sculpture romane d' Auvergne,* Clermont-Ferrand, 1978), le programme des sculptures de Notre-Dame du Port avait le même auteur que celui de Conques?

(25) Facsimilé du B, initiale du premier répons, dans Bruno Stäblein, *Schriftbild der einstimmi-gen Musik,* Leipzig, 1975 [Musikgeschichte in Bildern, Band III, Lieferung 4], Abb.35.

(26) Facsimilé des neumes dans S. Corbin *Die Neumen,* Köln, 1977, Tafel 26. Dans *Musicologie médiévale : Neumes et Séquences, Actes de la Table ronde de paléographie musicale à Orléans-La Source,* Paris, 1986, pl. IV. Cf. Louis Brou *L' ancien Office de saint Vaast évèque d' Arras : Etudes grégoriennes,* IV, 1961, p.7—42.

(27) Vaticane Regin. 577, ff.91v—94 : cf. Mgr. P. Villetard, *Offices de saint Savinien et de saint Potentien. Texte et chant publiés d' après le ms. d'Odoranne (XI—XIIe siécle),* Paris, 1956 [Bibliothèque musicologique, V].

(28) Angers, Bibl. municipale 814; Paris, B.N. lat. 9376, fragment d'office propre ; lat. 11574, f. l.

(29) Paris, B.N. lat. 3778, f.174—179 : *Catal.codd. hag. Paris.* I (1889) p. 238—270 ; lat. 5344, f.54 et ss. : *ibid.* II, p.270—271.

(30) J. Hourlier, *Extension du culte de St. Rémy en Italie : Etudes grégoriennes* I, 1954, p.181—185 : cette étude se base sur l'analyse des mss de Montecassino 494, Naples, Bibl. Naz. VIII B 51 et enfin Vercelli CCV.

(31) Au IXe siècle, les *Ordines romani* circulaient à l' état isolé avant d'être intégrés dans des collections, ainsi par exemple l'*Instructio ecclesiastici ordinis* (= l'Ordo L de l'édition de Mgr. M. Andrieu), qui était au IXe siècle contenue dans un *codicillo :* cf. P. Lehman, *Mittelalterliche Bibliothekskataloge . . .* I, München, 1918, p. 71.

(32) Paris, Bibl. Mazarine 525 : cf. S. Corbin, *Répertoire des mss. médiévaux contenant des notations musicales.* II, *Bibliothèque Mazarine* (Paris, 1966), p. 35—36 et pl. VI.

(33) Paris, B.N. lat. 2984 A, f. 87 — 104v.

(34) *Tropen- und Sequenzenhandschriften.* München, 1964, R I S M. B V 1

(35) Cf. R. Weakland, « The Beginnings of Troping » : *Musical Quarterly* 44, (1958), p.477—488 ; M. Huglo, « Aux origines des tropes d'interpolation : le trope méloforme d'introït » : *Revue de musicologie* LXIV (1978), p.12.

(36) A propos du t. 3 du *Corpus Troporum* j'ai évoqué dans *Scriptorium* (XXXVIII, 1984, p. 168) l'interêt du procédé de description en ces termes : « L'ordre des tropes pour une même fête est toujours différent d'une église à une autre, mais se perpétue parfois identique dans les mss. d'un même centre (par ex. Bénévent, voir p. 258, 261 etc., mais exception à la p. 275). On se rend très bien compte de cette loi en consultant les tableaux des pp. 256 et ss. où on peut constater que le fameux trope-dialogue *Quem quaeritis* vient en tête de liste dans les mss français, anglais et dans quelques allemands anciens, parfois avec une belle initiale tandis qu' au début de la tradition sangallienne . . . il vient en fin de liste puis disparait aux XIe et XIIe siècles . . . ».

(37) Voir les travaux de Günther Weiss et de David G. Hughes cités dans mes *Tonaires* p. 131, note l.

(38) Cf. G. Fransen, *Les décrétales et les collections de décrétales* dans la Typologie des Sources du Moyen-Age occidental, n° 10.

(39) Parmi les mss de comput attribué à Helpericus d' Auxerre — sur lesquels Ludwig Traube avait fait naguère une profonde enquête — il faut remarquer le Paris, B.N. lat. 7361, intitulé au f.9v — donc au verso du deuxième quaternion du recueil ! — qui porte le titre « Incipit libellus Helprici de arte calculatoria ».

(40) L'enquête sur les mss « scientifiques » du Moyen-Age entreprise dans cette perspective serait très fructueuse.

(41) Sur la séquence primitive, voir plus haut ; sur la séquence rythmée et rimée, il faudrait ici encore analyser les petites collections isolées ajoutées à des mss non liturgiques. Lorsque Abélard adressa son sermonnaire à Héloïse, il lui rappela qu'il lui avait envoyé les six planctus dans un libellus : « Libello quondam hymnorum vel sequentiarum a me nuper precibus tuis consummato . . . » P.L. CLXXVIII, c.379 (cf. mes remarques à ce propos dans les *Cahiers de civilisation médiévale* XXII, 1979, p.357).

Gunilla Iversen

Pax et Sapientia

A Thematic Study on Tropes from Different Traditions

(Based primarily on Sanctus and Agnus Dei Tropes)

Are there any themes in trope texts which can be regarded as characteristic for tropes of a certain genre? Or for tropes from a certain regional tradition, limited in place and time? Or for a specific monastic tradition? These questions are the starting points of this article in which tropes will be studied from a thematical point of view.

In the rich literary heritage of biblical and patristic texts, of theological and liturgical treatises as well as hymns and other poetic creations there is a broad common textual basis on which composers of tropes and sequences depended. The writings of St. Augustine, St. Ambrose, Bede, Isidore and St. Jerome can, of course, be recognized echoing through trope texts from all regional traditions. On the other hand one can observe that certain themes and formulas are preferred in one tradition more than in another and that certain forms of expression fit into local theological, liturgical and aesthetic traditions better than others. To try to identify and to define a few such thematical preferences will be the purpose of this article.

In this study, which should be regarded as a pilot study, we will present a few selected central traits in the tropes to the Agnus Dei and the Sanctus in manuscripts dating from the tenth to twelfth century. The following four major textual themes will be treated:

1. *Pax, lux et sapientia* (Abstract nouns as epithets in the Western tradition)
2. *Trinitas et unitas* (Trinitarian themes in the late Northwestern tradition)
3. *Haec festa praecelsa/convenite omnes* (Introductions in the Aquitanian tradition)
4. *Salva et parce/quos redimisti cruore* (Prayers in the Italian traditions)

1. PAX, LUX ET SAPIENTIA

Abstract epithets as invocations in the Western tradition

In the Western tradition, the Agnus Dei tropes are above all songs praising Christ the Lord. In the Northwest they are even rubricated as LAUDES — which in fact they are. In the Winchester troper Ox 775, where the different sections of Ordinary tropes have rubrics in hexameters, the Sanctus tropes have:

INCIPIUNT LAUDES AD DULCIA CANTICA SANCTUS

And the Agnus Dei tropes are introduced with the following rubric:

INCIPIUNT LAUDES RESONANT QUAE DULCITER AGNUM

QUI VENIENS PECCATA PIUS TULIT IMPIA MUNDI[1]

But most importantly, a large number of ordinary tropes in the North West present theological expressions defining God primarily with abstract nouns such as *pax, lux* and *sapientia,* peace, light and wisdom. In this they illustrate their dependence on a long patristic tradition of theological thinking and stylistic method — as we will try to demonstrate below.

Trope elements as invocations

Let us first observe the main structure of the troped Agnus Dei in the Western tradition.[2] This is what could be regarded as a "typical" way of combining base text and trope elements in this tradition:

Agnus dei qui tollis peccata mundi miserere nobis.

Trope element	*Miserere nobis.*
Trope element	*Miserere nobis.*
(Trope element	*Miserere nobis.)*
(Trope element	*Miserere nobis.)*

. . .

The liturgical base text is given once *in extenso*. After this there follows a varying number of trope elements as invocations addressed to the Lord and ending in the repeated supplication of *miserere nobis* (and *dona nobis pacem* as the final supplication in chants dating from the latter part of the eleventh century). The main structure of the Agnus Dei chant in the Western tradition before the end of the eleventh century differs from the Eastern and Italian traditions. On the other hand, it is similar to the structure of another liturgical text found in contemporary sources, the Litany of Saints:

Gallican Litany of Saints:[3]

. . .

Pater de caelis, deus, *miserere nobis.*
Filius, redemptor, deus, *miserere nobis.*
Spiritus sanctus, deus, *miserere nobis.*
Sancta dei trinitas, *miserere nobis.*
Qui es trinus et unus, *miserere nobis.*
Ipse idemque benignus, *miserere nobis.*

. . .

Like the Agnus Dei, this litany is built of invocations ending in the supplication *miserere nobis.* The Trinitarian formula addressing God the Father, the Son, the Holy Spirit and the Trinity, recalls formulas used in the tropes in the same Western tradition — as we will see below (p. 33ss). The phrase beginning with *Qui es* in the litany has an equivalent in, for instance, the following trope to the Agnus Dei, which is found in sources from Winchester, Cambrai, Le Mans and Saint Evroult:

> *Agnus dei qui tollis peccata mundi, miserere nobis.*
> Qui es vera sapientia
> et verbum et virtus patris, *Miserere nobis.*
> Qui sedes ad dexteram dei
> maiestatis in excelsis, *Miserere nobis.*
> (CT IV, 75)

The trope text varies the invocation of the liturgical base text, calling upon the one who is "the true Wisdom and Word and Power of the Father". It is notable how Christ is given three abstract epithets in this invocation. It takes up a range of biblical expressions, *verbum, virtus* and *sapientia* (I Cor. 1,18; John 1,1 . . . etc.) The last invocation is also biblical (Hbr 1,3), addressing the one, "who sits in the Father's right side in heavenly majesty". By the phrase *qui sedes ad dexteram dei,* it recalls the *Gloria in excelsis.* The same structure, with trope elements used as invocations, is found in the majority of Agnus Dei tropes from Western sources. In the following two examples, the structure and function of the trope elements are the same, though here in the form of hexameters:

> *Agnus dei qui tollis peccata mundi miserere nobis.*
> Qui patris in solio residens per saecula regnans, *miserere nobis.*
> Tu pax, tu pietas, bonitas, miseratio clemens, *miserere nobis.*
> Singula discutiens, dum sederis arbiter orbis, *miserere nobis.*
> (CT IV, 76)

Here Christ is not only addressed as King and Judge but also as Peace, Piety, Tenderness and Mild Mercy.

Abstract epithets

In a similar way, abstract nouns are of crucial importance in a large number of texts from the Northwestern region. In the following example, a trope found in both Northwestern and Aquitanian repertories, Christ is called upon as Eternal Wisdom and True Light of the True Light:

> *Agnus dei qui tollis peccata mundi, miserere nobis.*
> Omnipotens aeterna dei sapientia, Christe, *miserere nobis.*
> Verum subsistens vero de lumine lumen, *miserere nobis.*
> Optima perpetuae concedens gaudia vitae, *miserere nobis.*
> (CT IV, 63)

In the Northwestern version of this trope Christ is addressed as almighty eternal wisdom, *aeterna* being an attribute of *sapientia,* thus emphasizing the importance of *sapientia.* In the Aquitanian version on the other hand the corresponding reading is *aeterne* — *Omnipotens aeterne, dei sapientia, Christe,* thus connecting *aeterne* with *omnipotens* as in the formula used in the prayers beginning with these words.

The next two examples, both hexameters with internal rhymes dating from the late eleventh century, follow the same tradition:

> *Agnus dei qui tollis peccata mundi,*
> Omnipotens verbum patris deitate coaevum, *miserere nobis.*
> *Agnus dei qui tollis peccata mundi,*
> Vera salus hominum, firmissima spes miserorum, *miserere nobis.*
> *Agnus dei qui tollis peccata mundi,*
> Virtus cuncta creans, pax omnia iure serenans, *dona nobis pacem.*
> (CT IV, 66)

and:

> *Agnus dei qui tollis peccata mundi,*
> Lux lucis verbumque patris virtusque perennis, *miserere nobis.*
> *Agnus dei qui tollis peccata mundi,*
> Verus sanctorum splendor nosterque redemptor, *miserere nobis.*
> *Agnus dei qui tollis peccata mundi,*
> Nostra salus, pax vera, deus, altissima virtus, *dona nobis pacem.*
> (CT IV, 56)

Here again we find series of abstract expressions used as invocations: *verbum, salus, spes, virtus* and *pax.*

In both tropes the abstract nouns are expanded by means of nominal attributes in the genitive case or possessive pronouns as in *lux lucis, verbum patris, splendor sanctorum* and *nostra salus,* and/or in the form of adjective attributes as in *omnipotens verbum, verus splendor, pax vera* and *altissima virtus.*

As we can observe in the examples given above, the invocational phrases can be formed in principally three ways in this tradition: First, and not surprisingly, they can be formed as relative clauses recalling formulas used in prayers and in the *Gloria in excelsis*[4] as well as other liturgical and biblical texts — a form which might well be expected to be the "normal" and most frequent also in these trope texts: *qui: qui sedes ad dexteram patris, qui es vera sapientia* as in *Qui es vera.* The phrases can also have a present participle replacing the relative clause: *residens, regnans, subsistens, concedens, discutiens* as in *Qui patris* and in *Omnipotens aeterna dei.*

Mostly, however, — and this is particularly notable in tropes from the Northwestern region — the trope elements do not contain a verb, as in the trope elements *Tu pax tu pietas . . ., Omnipotens aeterna dei sapientia . . ., Omnipotens verbum . . ., Vera salus hominum . . ., Lux lucis . . ., Verus sanctorum splendor . . ., Nostra salus, pax vera, deus . . ., Sanctorum splendor . . .* and *Lux, via, vita, salus* etc.

Similar to the Gallican Litany (see above p. 25), the trope elements are composed as appositional phrases giving theological expositions of the very essence of the addressed divinity in a dense and compressed form. These texts do not address the Lamb of God as the sacrificed and risen redeemer of the world as much as the one who is *Pax et Sapientia, Lux et Verbum, Virtus et Pietas, Spes et Vita, Salus et Decus, Pietas, Bonitas et Miseratio* etc. Thus God is named in a series of abstract expressions. These words are frequently found in the repertories of Winchester, Durham, Arras, Cambrai, Le Mans, Saint Magloire and Saint Evroult, all representing the Northwestern tradition. And it is not only tropes to the Agnus Dei but also tropes to other genres from the same region that reflect this thematic tradition.

As we said above, certain traits discernable in the tropes to the Agnus Dei can also be observed in other tropes of other genres from the same tradition. Thus we may compare these with a trope to the Sanctus, e g. *Summe pater* found in manuscripts from St. Alban's, Reims and one of the Sicilian manuscripts that preserve a repertory from Normandy (Madrid B.N. ms 19421):

> *Sanctus.*
> Summe pater, deitatis amor, bone conditor orbis,
> *Sanctus.*
> Sanctorum splendor, decus inviolabile pacis,
> *Sanctus.*
> Quem chorus ecclesiae colit ac veneranter adorat.
> *Dominus deus Sabaoth.*
> Te dominum caeli clamat iubilatio sancta.
> *Pleni sunt caeli et terra gloria tua.*
> *Osanna in excelsis.*
> Lux, via, vita, salus, tibi psallimus omne per aevum.
> *Benedictus qui venit (in nomine domini*
> *Osanna in excelsis)*[5]

This Sanctus trope addresses God as Father and Creator but most explicitly in abstract nouns: *amor, sanctorum splendor, decus inviolabile pacis* — the Love of God, the splendour of the saints, the impeccable beauty of peace. In the last trope element "we bring praises for ever to you, the Light, the Way, the Life and the Salvation". Here the Lord is addressed exclusively in abstract nouns: *Lux, via, vita, salus . . .*

In a Kyrie trope found in manuscripts from Cambrai and Arras[6], the following phrase is found as an invocation in the second section of the chant:

> Lux, via, vita, salus, spes, pax, sapientia, virtus,
> nos te rogamus, eleyson: *Christe eleyson.*

This trope element contains an even longer list of enumerated names, by the words *spes, pax, sapientia* and *virtus,* all abstract nouns.

These trope texts recall the formula used in another liturgical text; that of the *contestatio,* the Preface in the versified *Missa Gallicana* edited by Mone from a manuscript dating from around 700.

After the beginning *Dignum* phrase we find *Lux, via, vita, decus . . .:*

> *Alia contestatio*
> Dignum, aequum ac iustum est, tibi nos, pie, clangere laudes.
> Lux, via, vita, decus, spes, fons, sator, arbiter, auctor,
> Gratia, dulcedo, sapientia, gloria, regnum.
> Qui sine principio perstas, sine fine per aevum,
> Cuius trinus apex statuit tria maxima rerum,
> Sol, luna, astra, polus radiarunt lumine mundum,
> Fons, pecus, herba, frutex terras variavit honore,
> Piscis, concha, lapis, sal, murex aequora complet.[7]
> . . .

It is interesting to observe how these trope texts reflect their dependence on a long patristic tradition, treating the same themes and using the same vocabulary. Let us just recall a few examples from the rich literary tradition to which this kind of trope text belongs. Apart from the biblical sources (Io 1,1—14; Ps 35,10) the Credo and the prayers[8], the trope *Lux lucis* recalls a hymn by St. Ambrose from the fourth century:

> Splendor paternae gloriae
> De luce lucem proferens
> Lux lucis et fons luminis
> Dies dierum illuminans[9]

The trope texts in this Western tradition reflect such expositions on the names of Christ as the one composed by Rhabanus Maurus around 800, when he writes:

Verbum autem ideo dicitur, quia per eum omnia Pater condidit sive iussit;
Veritas, quia non fallit, sed tribuit quod promisit;
Vita, quia omnia vivificat; . . .
Virtus, quod omnem Patris potestatem in semet ipso habe[a]t et omnia potest;
Sapientia, quod ipse revelet mysteria scientiae et arcana sapientiae;
Splendor, quod manifestat;
Lumen, quia illuminat;
Lux, quia veritatem contemplandam cordis oculos reserat; . . .[10]

In a similar way Florus of Lyons writes in his versified transformation of St. John's Gospel in the ninth century:

Verbum Unigenitum semper cum Patre manebit.
Hic lux, hic virtus, hic est sapientia Patris,
Vita hominum, angelicis lucens super aethera turmis . . .[11]

And Sedulius Scotus in the same century begins his *Oratio contra falsidicos testes* with the following hexameter:

Lux aeterna, deus, fons lucis, fons veritatis[12]
. . .

In the trope texts which we have cited above, the names of the Lord have been almost exclusively *abstract* nouns such as *lux, pax* and *sapientia*. But there are also examples in which the Lord is addressed with *concrete* nouns, used both as symbols and metaphors. This also follows a long tradition, as for instance in the following two hexameters by Ennodius from around 500. Here abstract and concrete nouns appear side by side:

Fons, vis, dextra, lapis, vitulus, leo, lucifer, agnus,
Ianua, spes, virtus, verbum, sapientia, vates.[13]

Let us return to the texts in the trope manuscripts from Saints Evroult. In the repertory of this manuscript there is the interesting Sanctus trope *Trinitas, unitas, deitas*. This intriguing trope is worth a study of its own, but it must be quoted here as a further example of enumerations of names favoured in the trope[14] texts of this tradition. Its origin, however, is still obscure. This is the version in Saint Evroult:

Sanctus, Sanctus, Sanctus . . .

Osanna

1a Trinitas,	1b Maiestas,
unitas,	potestas,
deitas	claritas
superna,	aeterna,
2a Lapis, mons,	2b Sol, lumen,
petra, fons,	et numen,
flumen, pons,	cacumen,
semita,	et vita,
3a Tu sator,	3b Tu nitor
creator,	et decor,
amator,	et candor.
redemptor,	Tu splendor
salvator	et odor,
et vitae gaudia,	quo vivunt mortua,
4a Tu vertex	4b Quem laudant,
et apex,	adorant,
regum rex,	cui cantant,
legum lex,	quem amant,
et iudex,	quem clamant,
Tu laus angelica,	agmina caelica,
5a Tu theos,	5b Tu deus,
Tu heros,	Tu iustus,
dive flos,	Tu sanctus,
vive ros,	Tu bonus,
salva nos,	Tu rectus,
rege nos,	Tu pius,
perduc nos,	Tu clemens,
ad thronos	Tu summus
superos	dominus,
et vitae ianua.	Tibi sit gloria.

in excelsis.[15]

We will return to the Trinitarian theme of this text. Let us for the moment just observe the constellation of abstract and concrete nouns, and the delicate and well disposed order of the names.

In the same manuscript, Pa 10508, we also find the hexameter sequence *Alma chorus domini* which is a text built up of names in the same way:

De nominibus domini:
Alma chorus Domini nunc pangat nomina summi:
Messias soter, Emanuel, Sabaoth, Adonai
Est unigenitus, via, vita, manus, homousion,
Principium, primogenitus, sapientia, virtus,
Alpha, caput finisque simul vocitatur et est ω,
Fons et origo boni, paraclitus ac mediator,
Agnus, ovis, vitulus, serpens, aries, leo, vermis,
Os, verbum, splendor, sol, gloria, lux et imago,
Panis, flos, vitis, mons, ianua, petra lapisque,
Angelus et sponsus pastorque, propheta, sacerdos,
Athanatos, kyrios, theos pantocrator, Iesus.
Salvificet nos, sit cui saecla per omnia doxa.[16]

This sequence is found in a number of manuscripts in the West Frankish region. Blume and Bannister were unwilling to ascribe it to Notker due to its absence in the East Frankish manuscripts which contain sequences attributed to Notker and in which they would have expected to find it if it were a Notkerian sequence.

Regarding the structure and the vocabulary of this sequence, one is tempted to support the assumption that it rather originates from a West Frankish tradition in which the same themes of Christ as *lux, via, vita, virtus, verbum* and *sapientia* are essential and central in trope texts as well.

2. TRINITAS ET UNITAS

The Trinitarian theme in the North West

The Trinitarian theme, treated in theological expositions, subject of intense discussion, is reflected in tropes from the Western tradition especially. In tropes found in manuscripts from the second half of the eleventh century, the Trinitarian theme becomes more and more frequent. The trope texts reflect the same thoughts as were expressed a century earlier by, for instance, Hincmar of Reims in this treatise against Gottschalk's *De una et non trina trinitate.* Quoting scriptural passages and patristic discussions of the Trinity, he collects a massive quantity of material on the subject, defending the unity of the Trinity against Gottschalk, as in the following passage:

> *Deitas autem, qui Patrem Deum dicimus, Filium Deum dicimus, Spiritum Deum dicimus, et sono et intellectu singularis est numeri, et adjectionem pluralitatem significantem non recipit: quoniam sancta et inseparabilis in personis intelligitur et dicitur Trinitas et in substantia, essentia, natura, divinitate, deitate, intelligitur et dicitur unitas, quia deitas Trinitatis est unitas . . .*[17]

Again, the Sanctus trope *Trinitas unitas deitas,* presented above, expresses the same understanding of the Trinity in its first few lines:

> Trinitas, unitas, deitas superna,
> Maiestas, potestas, claritas aeterna . . .

As Karlheinz Schlager has pointed out, the melodies of this trope/sequence are entirely built up of threefold melodic figures illustrating the idea of the Trinity in the melodic form.[18]

Hincmar of Reims even gives an explanation of the significance of the words *pax* and *lux* as definitions of the Trinity. By their three letters they illustrate the threefold nature of the divinity:

> . . . et hoc *pacis* et *lucis* praecelsum vocabulum sanctae Trinitati convenientissime coaptatur: nimirum quod ex tribus litteris constat, et pluralitatis numerum sicut Deus ignorat. Cum enim dicimus *pax, lux,* per tres litteras tres in Deo personae intelliguntur, et quia *pax,* sicut nec *lux,* numerum pluralem non recipit, per singularem numerum substantia, id est deitas ipsius Dei accipitur . . .[19]

And Hincmar, is, of course, only one example of many in the rich variety of similar treatises on the Trinity.

The central place of the Trinitarian theme in the liturgical texts, in tropes, hymns and sequences illustrates its central place in the theological and liturgical discussions in the eleventh century, as the feast of the Trinity was still in process of being introduced as a separate feast in the liturgical year.[20]

A text ascribed to Bede, to Alcuin as well as to St. Hilary expresses the Trinitarian theme in phrases which can be recognized as trope elements. Let us quote just a section:

> . . .
>
> | | |
> |---|---|
> | Pater et Filius et Spiritus sanctus, | O beata Trinitas. |
> | Deus, Dominus, Paraclitus, | O beata Trinitas. |
> | Caritas, gratia, communicatio. | O beata Trinitas. |
> | Caritas deus est, | |
> | Gratia Christus, | |
> | Communicatio Spiritus sanctus, | O beata Trinitas. |
> | Genitor, genitus, regenerans, | O beata Trinitas. |
> | Verum lumen, | |
> | verum lumen ex lumine, | |
> | vera illuminatio, | O beata Trinitas. |
> | Invisibilis, invisibiliter, | |
> | visibilis, invisibiliter, | |
> | invisibilis, visibiliter, | O beata Trinitas. |
> | Fons, flumen, irrigatio, | O beata Trinitas. |
> | Ab uno omnia, | |
> | per unum omnia, | |
> | in uno omnia, | O beata Trinitas. |
> | A quo, per quem et in quo omnia, | O beata Trinitas. |
> | Vivens vita, | |
> | Vita a vivente, | |
> | Vivificator viventium, | O beata Trinitas.[21] |
>
> . . .

The *adnominatio* of *genitor, genitus, regenerans* as well as the *adnominatio* playing with the words *lumen ex lumine, invisibilis, visibiliter* are found in a number of Sanctus tropes. The common threefold form *de/ex quo, per quem, in quo* used in the formula of the preface and repeated twice in Bede's text, is found in different forms in the tropes as well.

In the Sanctus tropes the trinitarian form is naturally existant in the song from the beginning, the Sanctus invocations being normally addressed to the Father, the Son and the Holy Spirit in tropes from all traditions. Still, it seems to be more explicitly exposed in tropes from this region. Thus, for example, the following short Sanctus trope, here quoted from the manuscript from Saint Evroult, is built up on the formula *ex quo, per quem, in quo* mentioned above:

> *Sanctus,*
> Pater, ex quo omnia, deus.
> *Sanctus,*
> Filius, per quem omnia, deus.
> *Sanctus, dominus,*
> Spiritus, in quo omnia, colendus,
> *Deus Sabaoth.*
> *Pleni sunt caeli et terra gloria tua,*
> *Osanna in excelsis . . .*[22]

In the same manuscript, the theme is also expressed as follows:
> *Sanctus,*
> Summe pater, de quo mundi principia constant.
> *Sanctus,*
> Filius omnipotens, per quem patris est pie velle.
> *Sanctus,*
> Spiritus, in quo par virtus sine fine refulget.
> *Dominus deus Sabaoth,*
> *Pleni sunt caeli et terra gloria tua,*
> *Osanna in excelsis . . .*[23]

Exactly the same trope elements are used in an Agnus Dei trope in the same manuscript:

> *Agnus dei qui tollis peccata mundi, miserere nobis.*
> Summe pater, de quo mundi principia constant, *miserere nobis.*
> Filius unigenitus, per quem patris est pie velle,*miserere nobis.*
> Spiritus, in quo par virtus sine fine refulget, *dona nobis pacem.*
> (CT IV, 87)

Here the invocations addressed to the Father, the Son and the Holy Spirit end in supplications for mercy and peace.

Both tropes have the same melody: the only difference is that the variants *unigenitus* and *omnipotens* produce variations in the melody — *unigenitus* is one syllable longer than *omnipotens* — in fact one syllable too long to make a correct hexameter.

In the trope manuscript from Saint Evroult, we also find the following Agnus Dei trope:

> *Agnus dei qui tollis peccata mundi, miserere nobis.*
> Triplex personis, simplex deus esse sub uno, *miserere nobis.*
> Summe bonus, qui semper eras semperque manebis, *dona nobis pacem.*
> (CT IV, 88)

Here the *trinitas unitas* theme is expressed in the words *triplex — simplex —sub uno esse:* "threefold in persons, one God in one essence." Whereas the trinitarian theme, inherent from the beginning in the threefold exclamation *Sanctus, Sanctus, Sanctus,* is present in these tropes from all regions and all traditions, the *Agnus Dei* tropes are not primarily trinitarian, not even when added to a threefold chant.

In the Northwestern tradition towards the end of the eleventh century, there is, however, a notable tendency towards accomodating the Agnus Dei tropes to the Trinitarian theme. We have already seen one example in the trope *Summe pater de quo,* used as both Agnus and Sanctus trope, and in the trope *Triplex personis.* But it is not only in newly composed tropes that the trinitarian theme becomes more and more important during this period. One can also observe how old tropes are changed into a trinitarian form in the Northwestern tradition after 1050. This, for instance is the case with the well known trope *Christe redemptor.*[24] This trope is found both in the early Western and in the early Eastern tradition. In Prüm, Saint Magloire and Nevers it has the following form:

> *Agnus dei qui tollis peccata mundi, miserere nobis.*
> Christe redemptor
> orbisque factor,   *miserere nobis.*
> Omnipotens pater
> pius et clemens,
> magnus et magnificus,   *miserere nobis.*
> (CT IV, 43)

It is a trope to Christ as Redeemer and Creator of the world, and at the same time to the almighty Father, good and merciful, grand and magnificent.

When the same trope is inserted into the repertory of tropers from Saint Evroult and Normandy, from the end of the eleventh century, it is changed into a Trinitarian text:

Agnus dei qui tollis peccata mundi,
Omnipotens pater,
pius et clemens,
magnus et magnificus,
miserere nobis.
Agnus dei qui tollis peccata mundi,
Christe redemptor,
orbisque factor,
miserere nobis.
Agnus dei qui tollis peccata mundi,
Spiritus in cunctis radians et cuncta reformans,
dona nobis pacem.

The main structure is changed into the normalized threefold form and the last supplication is changed into *dona nobis pacem*. The order of the trope elements is reversed. The text is no longer christocentric: the first element addresses the Father almighty, the second the Son, Christ, the Redeemer. A third element in hexameter has been added: "Holy Spirit radiant in all and reforming all." In this way it is transformed into a Trinitarian trope corresponding to the literary and theological demands of this time and region . . .

3. HAEC FESTA PRAECELSA / CONVENITE OMNES

Introductions in Aquitanian tradition

In the Southwestern tradition, mainly represented in Aquitania, the Agnus Dei is generally introduced by a trope element. The main structure of the chant can then be described by the following model:

Trope element (= Introduction)
Agnus dei qui tollis peccata mundi, miserere nobis.
Trope element   *Miserere nobis.*
(Trope element   *Miserere nobis.)*
(Trope element   *Miserere nobis.)*[25]

For the moment we will focus only on the introductory trope element. This text, notably important in the Aquitanian tradition, functions generally as a sort of "Aufforderung zum . . .", inviting the singers to come together to perform the chant with joyful voice. But it also has a significant function in announcing the theme of the feast to be celebrated, or the theme of the text of the Ordinary chant. It underlines the specific liturgical *hic et nunc*.

This function is not only found in the introduction to the Agnus Dei but also in tropes to other Ordinary chants as well as in Proper tropes, as may be seen in the following examples:

Venite fratres in unum
Collaudemus dominum,
quia ipse est
Agnus dei qui tollis peccata mundi
. . .
(CT IV, 65)

This is an exhortation to the brothers to "come together to praise the Lord, because he is the Lamb of God" . . . By the phrase *quia ipse est* the invitation to sing leads to a smooth transition into the liturgical base text.

Another introduction reads:

Haec festa praecelsa
convenite omnes
sacrum corpus percipere
una voce proclamantes:
Agnus dei qui tollis peccata mundi, miserere nobis.
. . .
(CT IV, 52)

Here the invitation to "come together to receive the sacred host", *sacrum corpus percipere,* underlines the liturgical situation, the *hic et nunc* of the Agnus Dei chant in the mass. Its function here is close to that of the fraction antiphon sung during the Breaking of Bread and successively "replaced" by the Agnus Dei during this period.[26] Even the phrases *convenite omnes, sacrum corpus percipere* in the trope recall similar phrases in the Easter fraction antiphon used in the same region: *Venite populi ad sacrum et immortale mysterium . . . cum angelis clamantes Alleluia.*[27]

The ending of the introduction trope element *Haec festa praecelsa, una voce clamantes,* leads naturally to the phrase of the liturgical base text *Agnus Dei . . .*

In fact, this trope element introduces three different Agnus Dei tropes: *Agnus — eia et eia, Cuius in Aegyptum* and *Miserere super nos.*[28] In the same region, but in slightly different form, it is also used as an introduction to the communion antiphon for Easter:

Haec est festa praecelsa.
Convenite omnes
sacrum corpus percipere
una voce proclamantes:
Pascha nostrum . . .
(CT III, 108)

The opening phrase figures in similar versions in introit tropes to other feasts as well:

Haec est praeclara dies
tribus sacrata miraculis,
in qua cum propheta canamus
dicentes:
Ecce advenit dominator dominus . . .
(CT I, 103)

The trope element introduces the introit antiphon at Epiphany and the three miracles referred to in the introduction are, of course, the baptism of Christ, the adoration of the Magi and the miracle of Cana.

As we have seen, introductions to a chant of the Ordinary, as the Agnus Dei, can function as invitations to sing, and as introductions to the liturgical base text. But they can also function as a sort of "Proper" of the Ordinary, illustrating the theme of the actual feast.

In the earlier repertory in the Aquitanian manuscripts, dating from before 1300, there are a few introductions of this kind at the largest feasts of the year: Christmas, Easter, Pentecost and the feast of John the Baptist, adapting the Agnus Dei to the theme for the day.

Thus, at Easter we find the following introduction in Aquitanian manuscripts:

Pro cunctis deductus
ad immolandum fuisti ut agnus.
Redempta plebe captiva
te laeti deposcimus voce praecelsa:
Agnus dei qui tollis peccata mundi miserere nobis.

. . .

(CT IV, 68)

At the feast of John the Baptist, the Aquitanian version of the trope *Quem Iohannes* introduces the base liturgical text:

Quem Iohannes in Iordane baptizavit
ovans et dicens: ecce
Agnus dei qui tollis peccata mundi,
miserere nobis.
Cui Abel iustus atque sanctus
agno agnum obtulit immaculatum,
miserere nobis.
(CT IV, 69)

The first trope element recalls the passage in Jo 1,29 in which John the Baptist, on the bank of the river Jordan, points at Jesus saying the words which actually form the liturgical text: *Ecce Agnus Dei, ecce qui tollit peccatum mundi.*

Here *ecce* is inserted in the trope text, and by the words *ovans et dicens ecce* the phrase *Agnus dei . . .* is anticipated in a similar way as in the earlier examples, *una voce cantantes . . .,* and *quia ipse est . . .*

The second trope element alludes to the text of Genesis in which Abel prefigures Christ in three ways: as the shepherd guarding his sheep, as the one who brings his offering of a lamb to God, and finally as the one who is himself slaughtered like a lamb. Also in this element the liturgical *hic et nunc* is underlined by the reference to Abel as *justus et sanctus,* thus recalling the formula used in the Canon of the Eucharist. (We will return to this piece in considering the Italian trops, p. 49).

Another example of introduction forming a "Proper of the Ordinary" can be taken from the Sanctus repertory. In a number of early Aquitanian manuscripts, we find the following trope at Easter:

> Gloriosa dies adest,
> qua surrexit praepotens ex mortuis.
> Omnes dicite, eia:
> *Sanctus.*
> Idem deus conditor hominum
> factus est redemptor die ista.
> Laudem dicite, eia:
> *Sanctus.*
> Iam "Gloria in excelsis"
> cantant sancta agmina.
> Hymnum dicite, eia:
> *Sanctus dominus deus Sabaoth . . .*[29]

Here again we find expressions indicating the specific theme of the feast: *Gloriosa dies adest,* "the glorious day is here", with further explanation given in the relative clause. In the second element is the expression *die ista,* "this very day", on which the creator was made redeemer. (We will return to the exhortations to sing.)

A similar text is used to introduce the introit antiphon for the feast of St. Stephen in Pa 1084c:[30]

> Gloriosa dies haec,
> qua processit potens ex virginis aula.
> Idem deus conditor hominum
> factus est homo die ista.
> Iam "Gloria in excelsis"
> cantant[es] sancta agmina.
> Regi nato hoc quoque
> personet simul vox nostra.

With the introit the introduction is adapted to the themes of Christmas by the relative clause *qua processit potens ex virginis aula,* as well as by the reference to the *Gloria in excelsis,* this being primarily a Christmas hymn.

The phrase *gloriosa dies adest* corresponds to phrases like *Haec festa prae-celsa, Haec est festa praeclara* and *Haec est praeclara dies* above, and similar expressions are found in many other Aquitanian introductions:

Haec est nimis praefulgida festa . . .	Easter Fer. II intr.	(CT III, 108)
Haec est nimis praefulgida dies . . .	Easter Fer. II intr.	(CT III, 108)
Haec est dies valde praeclara . . .	Epiph. intr.	(CT I, 103)
Haec est praeclara dies . . .	Epiph. intr.	(CT I, 103)
etc.		

The ordinary main structure of the Sanctus is the one in which each of the three exclamations of Sanctus is followed by a trope element. In the case of the Sanctus trope *Gloriosa dies adest,* each of the three Sanctus acclamations is preceeded or introduced by trope elements, in which the exhortations *Omnes dicite eia, Laudem dicite eia* and *Hymnum dicite eia* directly lead to the Sanctus exclamation of the base text. This is very rare. I have not found any examples of such a structure outside Aquitania. But in the Aquitanian tradition this fits in very well. These expressions correspond to a large number of similar phrases in tropes of other genres in this tradition.

Psallite cum laude,		
cantate deo fratres,		
tempus adest, hora instat.		
Psallite iam nunc eia . . .	Pent. intr. (CT III, 166)	
*		
Omnes una voce cantemus . . .	Epiph. intr. (CT I, 112)	
*		
Eia cantate,		
eia, voce praecelsa dicentes . . .	Jo. Ev. off.	(CT I, 215)
*		
Filii carissimi, domino melos pangite		
una voce dicentes . . .	Innoc. intr.	(CT I, 94)
*		

(Vox clara personet . . ., clara voce . . ., voce praecelsa . . ., consona voce etc etc.)

The list could be made even much longer. Let us just note that in the tropes (as well as in the sequences, as has been shown by Lars Elfving in his study of the vocabulary of the sequences in Limoges)[31], phrases inviting the singers to sing joyfully are characteristic of the Aquitanian tradition. In the Preface preceeding the Sanctus in the mass, there are phrases introducing the Sanctus. These could make us expect similar phrases as introduction tropes as well. But as we have said they are not frequent as trope elements. One reason for their absence in the case of the Sanctus might perhaps be that the formulas of the different Prefaces already contain an introduction to the Sanctus. Let us recall the Gallican *contestatio* in the following two Prefaces:

"Ipsum igitur omnes angeli cum multiplici turba sanctorum
incessabili voce collaudant dicentes":
Sanctus, Sanctus, Sanctus . . .[32]
*

"Digne igitur ac iuste te laudare quem omnis angeli cumlaudant
et astra mirantur, maria benedicunt, terra veneratur, inferna suscipiunt,
cui cyryphym et seraphym non cessant clamare dicentes:"
Sanctus, Sanctus, Sanctus . . .[33]

There is one important difference between the phrases of the Preface introducing the Sanctus and the Aquitanian trope elements used as introductions. Whereas the words are put in the mouths of the Angels in the Preface — as they are in the biblical source — in the trope texts the central actors are the singers. The participants in the mass sing together with the prophet or with the words of the prophet:

Psallite omnes cum propheta dicentes	Epiph. off.	(CT I, 189)
Cum propheta canamus dicentes . . .	Epiph. intr.	(CT I, 103)
Gratulanter dicamus cum propheta . . .	Nat. III intr.	(CT I, 78)

But in the Italian traditions we recognize the expressions of the Preface as trope elements — as we will see below.

4. SALVA ET PARCE/QUOS REDEMISTI CRUORE

Tropes as prayers in Italian tradition

The Italian repertories are, as has been noticed lately, far more extensive than had previously been recognized.[34] Italian manuscripts dating from the later part of the eleventh century contain a rich treasure of tropes to the Agnus Dei and the Sanctus.[35] In the Italian traditions as a whole, the Agnus Dei tropes are not so much *"laudes"*, laudative invocations, as we have seen in the Western traditions, as they are *"preces"*.

There are many separate local traditions and it is not quite relevant to speak of only one main structure, or arrangement, of the troped Agnus Dei. Still, one can demonstrate the most frequent main structure by the following model:

Agnus dei qui tollis peccata mundi, miserere nobis.
Trope element
Agnus dei qui tollis peccata mundi, miserere nobis.
Trope element
Agnus dei qui tollis peccata mundi, miserere nobis.
Trope element[36]

The base liturgical text is repeated fully three times and the trope elements form a parallel threefold unit.

The following trope is found both in the Northern Italian and in the Southern Italian (Beneventan) traditions:

Agnus dei qui tollis peccata mundi, miserere nobis.
Benigne pater,
suscipe preces
ad te clamantes.

Agnus dei qui tollis peccata mundi, miserere nobis.
Agie proles,
tuos tuere,
quos redemisti cruore.

Agnus dei qui tollis peccata mundi, miserere nobis.
Sit tibi, nate,
gloria perpes
nunc et in aevum.
(CT IV, 41)

It is an intense prayer to Christ as the Father and Son, *pater* and *proles,* imploring to receive the prayers calling upon him, *preces ad te clamantes,* and to see to the supplicants, *tuos,* who are the ones Christ redeemed with his own blood, *quos redemisti cruore.* The final trope element is formed as the doxology of a prayer. The three trope elements form a parallel threefold unity beside the base liturgical text. Within the trope text of the first two elements is both an invocation, *Benigne pater* and *Agie proles,* and a supplication, *suscipe preces* and *tuos tuere.* We can compare this with the tradition in the Northwest in which we could observe how the trope elements normally only contained an invocation and where the supplication was expressed by the *miserere nobis* phrases of the base liturgical text. The final trope element in *Benigne pater* is formed as the doxology of a prayer: *sit tibi gloria nunc et in aevum,* with the additions *nate* and *perpes.* This trope can be seen as an example of a "typical" Italian trope to the Agnus Dei. In the following we will make further observations of what appears to be characteristic of the Agnus Dei and other tropes in Italy.

Discussing the main structure of the Agnus Dei in the Western tradition we compared it to the so called Gallican Litany. Likewise it seems relevant to relate the Italian Agnus Dei to the Roman Litany as well as to the Lombardian regarding their form and vocabulary. The Lombardic Litany, also called the Italian Litany, is found in manuscripts contemporary to the trope manuscripts, some of the earliest sources being in fact at the same time trope manuscripts. The actual section of the Italian Litany reads:

Agnus Dei qui tollis peccata mundi, miserere nobis.
Suscipe deprecationem nostram,
qui sedes ad dexteram Patris.
Gloria Patri et Filio et
Spiritui Sancto in saecula saeculorum.
Agnus Dei qui tollis peccata mundi, miserere nobis.[37]
. . .

The phrase *Agnus Dei qui tollis peccata mundi, miserere nobis* is given twice *in extenso*. The phrases *Suscipe deprecationem nostram* and *Qui sedes ad dexteram patris* recall the text of the *"Gloria in excelsis"*. These phrases all appear in tropes to the Agnus Dei in the Northern Italian (Lombardian) repertories. Thus in Northern Italy we find the tropes *Qui sedes ad dexteram patris/Qui es trinus, Qui sedes ad dexteram/Suscipe deprecationem, Qui sedes* and *Suscipe deprecationem*.[38]

In the Roman Litany the entire phrase *Agnus Dei qui tollis peccata mundi, miserere nobis* appears only once, but also here *in extenso:*

> Christe, audi nos
>
> . . .
>
> Propitius esto, parce nobis, domine.
> Propitius esto, libera nos, domine.
> Ab omni malo libera nos, domine.
> Per crucem tuam libera nos, domine.
> Peccatores te rogamus, audi nos.
> Ut pacem dones, te rogamus, audi nos.
> Filius dei, te rogamus, audi nos.
> *Agnus dei, qui tollis peccata mundi, miserere nobis.*[39]

This litany is expressedly christocentric, addressing Christ with the words *Christe, Domine, Filius Dei* and *te,* imploring Christ by his cross, *per crucem.* The supplications are not, as in the Gallican Litany, expressed by means of the repeated *miserere nobis,* but are formed by varying imperatives: *audi nos, propitius esto, parce nobis, libera nos* and by the final subjunctive *ut pacem dones.* The praying assembly is present in the text by the words *nos, nobis, peccatores te rogamus.* When returning to the trope texts in the Italian repertories we will recognize these specific formulations.

Again one could say that certain expressions and formal patterns which seem to be favoured in liturgical texts of one kind are also preferred in other liturgical texts in the same regional (or monastic) tradition. Thus, there is a notable resemblance in the form of the Agnus Dei and the form of the litany as they are reflected in the Western and Italian sources, where different forms of the liturgical texts appear to reflect different liturgical traditions and theological thinking, as well as different aesthetic preferences.

The short phrases

The striking difference between the Italian tropes and tropes from other traditions is the frequent use of very short paroxytone verses. The most common phrase consists of five syllables, two of them stressed, as in the rhythmic *adonius* (to use Dag Norberg's terminology[40]), or, as in the classical Roman *cursus planus* as in: *nunc et in aevum* and *cursus velox* as in *saecula saeculorum:* In the specific Roman contributions to the Roman mass, such as the prayers of the Canon, we recognize the same well documented characteristic trait. Let us observe a few examples from the Agnus Dei tropes:

Sit tibi nate	5 p
gloria perpes	5 p
nunc et in aevum	5 p (CT IV, 42)

* * *

Iuste et pie	5 p
atque benigne	5 p
concede nobis	5 p
veniam semper	5 p (CT IV, 47)

* * *

Tu qui iurasti	5 p
patribus nostris	5 p
dare nobis	4 p
vitam perennem	5 p (CT IV, 47)

* * *

Humanum genus	5 p
venisti salvare	6 p (CT IV, 54)

* * *

Agnus verus	4 p
immaculatus	5 p (CT IV, 40)

* * *

This tendency to form the text into short phrases is notably evident in the structure of the melodies which can be illustrated in the trope *Fulgida qui regnas*.[41] This Agnus Dei trope is found in two different versions, one in Northern Italian sources and one trope manuscript from Nevers, which is the earliest source of the trope. The other version is found in Beneventan sources. A comparison between the two versions helps us to observe how different aesthetic preferences affected the form and resulted in songs of very different character, though they contain almost identical texts.

The Beneventan version:

Agnus dei qui tollis peccata mundi, miserere nobis.
Fulgida qui regnas
in maiestate,
tute nobis tribue
semper laudare.

Agnus dei qui tollis peccata mundi, miserere nobis.
Alpha et O,
cui tripudiant
agmina sanctorum,
aeterna nobis
largire gaudia.

Agnus dei qui tollis peccata mundi, miserere nobis.
Ipse ad patriam
nos perduc atque
verae laetitiae
gaudia. Amen.

In the Beneventan version, text and music in all the elements are built up from short phrases. (See below). There is no obvious effort to form phrases with assonance. This can be compared with the Nevers version:

O lucis splendor,
angelorum cui canit concentus,
igne cor nostrum tuo adure, redemptor.
Agnus [dei qui tollis peccata mundi, miserere nobis.]
Fulgida qui regnas in maiestate,
tute nobis tribue semper laudare.
Miserere nobis.
Alpha et O,
cui tripudiant agmina sanctorum,
iocundos nos fac de praemio aeterno,
Dona nobis pacem.

Here the phrases are longer. There is no clear tendency to make short phrases. On the other hand the well documented tendency toward phrases built up with assonances and vocal rhymes in Aquitanian and West Frankish sequences and other poetry seems to be illustrated in this version of the trope. In the element *O lucis splendor* the dominant vowel is *o/u: O,* lucis, splendor, cor, nostrum, tuo, adure, redemptor;

In the element *Fulgida qui regnas* there are the rhymes on *a — e* which are stressed whereas the melody creates a long line. (The Beneventan version also has short phrases in the melody.) In the third element, *Alpha et O,* the manuscript from Nevers has a version in which the vowel *o* is dominant: O sanctorum, iocundos, nos, praemio, aeterno and *aeterna nobis largire gaudia* in Benevento stands against *iocundos nos fac de praemio aeterno* in Nevers.

In a similar way we can compare the prosula/trope *Laudes deo* in another Southern Italian manuscript, (Vat 602) from Monte Cassino, and the manuscript from Nevers:

Nevers (Pa 9449):   Monte Cassino (Vat 602):
Sanctus, sanctus, sanctus,

Dominus deus Sabaoth,
Pleni sunt caeli et terra gloria tua,
Osanna in excelsis.
Benedictus qui venit in nomine domini,

44

O	*Sanctus.*
Laudes deo	Laudes deo
ore pio	ore pio
corde sereno,	corde sereno
concio, melos tinnulo:	carmine demus tinnulo.
O	*Sanctus.*
In iubilo	In iubilo
cum cantico	cum cantico
simul ad alta	simul in alto
resonet vox cum organo:	resonet vox cum organo.
O	*Sanctus Dominus deus Sabaoth.*
Alpha et O	Caeli regi,
puro carmine	terrae, marium,
necne dicito:	rerum omnium,
O	*Pleni sunt caeli et terra gloria.*
Patri almo,	*Osanna in excelsis.*
genito quoque	Patri almo,
flamini sancto.	genito quoque,
Osanna	flamini sancto,
Trino deo	*Benedictus qui venit in nomine domini.*
omnes proclamant	Alpha et O
In excelsis.	puro carmine
	necne dicitur.
	Trino deo
	omnes proclamant
	Osanna in excelsis.

In Nevers, as in a number of Northern Italian manuscripts, this text is a prosula to the *Osanna.* All phrases are built on the vowel *o,* thus playing on the *o* of the word *Osanna.* Only in the last phrase is there an echo of the vowels *a-a* in *Osanna,* the word *proclamant.*[42]

When the same text is used in the manuscript from Monte Cassino, it is divided into trope elements, which are inserted between the phrases of the whole Sanctus chant. The melody underlines the short phrases of four or five syllables, *laudes deo, ore pio,* or *corde sereno.* In the cases where the reading differs from the Northern version there is no notable tendency to retain the consequent rhymes on the vowel *o,* as can be seen in the trope element *Caeli regi* and the readings *carmine demus* in the first element and *necne dicitur* in the last.

Tropes as prayers

As we observed above, the Agnus Dei tropes are formed as intense prayers. Like *Benigne pater,* presented above, the tropes are principally built up of three or four themes that generally follow a pattern which could be summarized as follows:

1. *Exaudi nos,* "Hear us!", 2. *Qui redemisti nos sanguine tuo,* "Who redeemed us with your own blood", 3. *Salva nos et dona nobis gaudia aeterna,* "Save us and give us the joys of eternal life", or *Sit tibi gloria, Amen,* "Glory be to thee. Amen", a regular doxology. In the Agnus Dei tropes one element (often the first) is a plea to the Lord to hear the supplications of the congregation. The form of address is often the vocative form: *aeterne, agie, Agne Dei, benigne, alme, bone, Christe,* sometimes even preceeded by *O: O Christe piissime:*

> Benigne pater,
> suscipe, quaeso,
> ad te clamantes.   (CT IV, 41)
> * * *
>
> Conditor mundi,
> exaudi nos clemens.   (CT IV, 84)
> * * *
>
> Supplicum preces,
> benigne, exaudi.   (CT IV, 84)
> * * *
>
> Exaudi, domine,
> rex caelorum,
> populorum gemitus.   (CT IV, 49)
> * * *

Another element (often the second) will contain an allusion to the passion of Christ. For Christ is not only King of Kings, but above all, the one who died on the cross to save the world. The theme of *Christ as the sacrificial lamb,* who saved the world with his *blood* is frequent in the Italian tradition as a whole. In the Agnus Dei repertory and in the Beneventan manuscripts, it is even more stressed:

> Cruore tuo
> salvasti mundum   (CT IV, 40)
>
> Qui pro nostra salute
> patri in cruce
> sacrificium obtulisti   (CT IV, 62)

Qui pro nostra salute
pependisti in cruce   (CT IV, 62)

Qui morti claustra
resurgendo fregisti,
et salva et parce
quos redemisti,   (CT IV, 54)

tuos tuere,
quos redemisti cruore.   (CT IV, 41)

The central place of Christ as sacrificial lamb in the Italian Agnus Dei tropes may be related to the fact that the chant itself as a part of the Roman mass evidently has its origins in the liturgy of the Syrian Greeks in Sicily. Obviously it had been a part of the liturgy practiced in South Italy during the time before it was officially introduced into the mass by pope Serge I, who himself originated from the same area.[43]

One trope element concludes the prayer with expressions such as the following:

Ne constent nobis
peccatorum vitia,
quod resurgamus,
ne pereamus,   (CT IV, 54)

Or the final element expresses the prayer for eternal life:

Gaudia superna pacis
dona nobis benigne.   (CT IV, 44)
*

dare nobis
vitam perennem.   (CT IV, 47)
*

Largitor pacis,
pacem perpetuam
tribue nobis.   (CT IV, 49)

Often the trope ends with the word *Amen* as in the following example:

Ipse ad patriam
nos perduc atque
verae laetitiae
gaudia. Amen   (CT IV, 51)

And we remember the final doxology of the trope *Benigne pater:*

Sit tibi, nate,
gloria perpes
nunc et in aevum.   (CT IV, 42)

The trope elements form together a syntactical and textual unit which is more separate from the liturgical base text of the chant than is usual in the Agnus Dei chants in the Western tradition studied earlier.

In the Italian Litany, and even more in the Roman Litany of the Saints, we have seen how every separate phrase consists of both an invocation, *Christe, filius Dei, Domine* and a supplication *parce, libera,* etc.

The relation *TU — NOS* is notably accentuated in the Italian tropes. This lies of course in the nature of the direct prayer: *"We* pray to *You Who* have suffered for *us:* bring us your peace and salvation."

It is also notable that the Italian Agnus Dei tropes are explicitly christocentric in a way which differs from the texts of the Northwestern tradition studied above. Direct speech is addressed to Christ, *TU.* This direct speech is also expressed by a verb in the second person: *obtulisti, pependisti, fregisti, salvasti,* etc, as well as by imperative forms: *suscipe, tuere, parce, salva,* etc.

The short phrases in the trope texts also recall the short expressions used in a number of *Mozarabic preces* which occur in many Italian sources from the same period.[44] These *preces* are often built up of the same vocabulary as the trope texts, as exemplified by the following example of Mozarabic formulas:

Ad te clamantes,	Deus, exaudi.
Bone redemptor,	Deus, exaudi.
Contrito corde,	Deus, exaudi.
De tuis caelis,	Deus, exaudi.

* * *

Exaudi clamantes,	Pater altissime.
Ea quae precamur	clemens attribue.

* * *

Bone redemptor	supplices quaesumus.
De toto corde	flentes requirimus.[45]

The intense exhortations of the imperatives, *exaudi, attribue, assiste,* as well as the vocative forms, *altissime, bone,* and the expressions reflecting the presence of the supplicants in the text itself, *clamantes precamur, nos, supplices quaesumus, flentes requirimus,* are all found in trope texts, as we have noticed. The function of the two kinds of texts is obviously the same: that of a prayer. In cases where tropes from other traditions are inserted into the repertory one can sometimes observe how these tropes are transformed by additional trope elements of phrases to create a version of the trope in which the character of prayer is stressed. Or, an element may be added so that the central theme of the passion of Christ is underlined in the trope. This is the case with the trope

Quem Iohannes, which we encountered as a trope of two elements at the feast of John the Baptist in Aquitanian sources and which is found in all traditions in one form or another. In some Italian sources this trope has a third element recalling the passion:

> Qui pro nobis mortem pati voluisti,
> ut nos a morte perpetua liberares   (CT IV, 71)

"Who were willing to suffer death for our sake/to liberate us from eternal death." (Here quoted from the Monte Cassino Ms Vat 602). It is worth noting that in the cases where a version of this element is found in repertories outside Italy, in Metz, St. Evroult, Echternach and Prüm — all in the transitional zone — the crucial phrase *mortem pati* in the Italian version corresponds to the phrase *nasci pati.* There, Christ is praised not as the One who was willing to die, but as the One who was born for us . . .

In the tropes to the Sanctus one can, among other themes, observe the same preference to address Christ as the One who took human body to save the world with His blood. Thus there are in the Beneventan repertory a number of examples of tropes found in traditions outside Italy, but which are transformed, by additions, to express this theme. In a Beneventan manuscript (Ben 40) the Trinitarian Sanctus trope *Deus pater ingenitus,* which is a trope found in several different traditions, is provided with an additional trope element *Qui venisti carnem sumens,* inserted between *Benedictus — domini* and *Osanna in excelsis:*

Sanctus,
Deus pater ingenitus,
Sanctus,
Filius eius unigenitus,
Sanctus dominus,
Paraclitus ex utroque procedens,
Deus Sabaoth.
Pleni sunt caeli et terra gloria tua,
Osanna in excelsis.
Benedictus qui venit in nomine domini.
Qui venisti carnem sumens ex matre
pro totius mundi salute,
tu nos ab hoste potenter libera,
et exaudi cunctos famulos tuos,
ut possimus laudes promere tibi
voce indefessa.
Osanna in excelsis.[46]

Whereas the three trope elements added to the Sanctus exclamations are formed as plain invocations to the three persons of the Trinity, the additional text has a totally different character: it is entirely christocentric. Christ is called upon as the one who came to the world to take on human form and who died on the Cross for the salvation of the whole world *(qui venisti carnem sumens ex matre pro totius mundi salute),* and in the following phrase there is an intense prayer recalling the prayers that we have found in the Agnus Dei tropes both in Benevento and in the Northern Italian tradition as well. We recognize the *tu-nos* relation and the imperatives *libera, exaudi (famulos tuos),* "Liberate us, listen to *your* servants" and also the ending phrase, *ut possimus laudes promere tibi,* "so that we can bring praises to you." In other tropes to the Sanctus there are phrases of a similar kind. In the Beneventan manuscript Ben 34, a Sanctus containing no other trope elements, has the following text inserted into the final *Osanna in excelsis:*

Osanna
Pie Christe,
descendisti ad terram
mundum tua factura salvans.
Inferni claustra confregisti fortiter,
dira iura ipsa dextra conculcans,
sanctos sursum levans in aethra,
ut tibi laudes decantent
In excelsis.[47]

Again, this is a christocentric text, addressing in vocative form Christ as the "One who came down to earth to save the world by breaking down the prison of death, crushing its fearful power with your own right hand and lifting up the holy ones to the heaven". The final phrase, *ut tibi laudes decantent in excelsis,* "so that they (the holy ones) may bring praises to you in the Highest", takes up a theme to which we will return below, the praises of the angels, the Cherubim and the Seraphim . . .

To the *Sanctus* trope *Altissime creator,* which is found in other regions as well, the Beneventan manuscript Ben 34 adds the phrase, *quaesumus Christe / parce peccata nobis indignis,* "we beseech you, Christ, forgive our sins, although we are not worthy".[48] And in MC 546 and Vat 602 there is also the reading *Laxa peccata cuncta / Domine, miserere nobis* inserted into the same trope: "Take away all our sins./ Lord, have mercy upon us."[49] The praying assembly talking to, *imploring* Christ to help and save is present in the text. Certainly, we meet similar phrases also in tropes from other traditions, phrases in which the themes of the Incarnation and the Passion are expressed in similar ways (as in the late tropes from St. Gall for instance.) But the themes are never as predominant and accentuated; phrases like *sacrificium obtulisti, mortem pati voluisti, qui venisti carnem sumens* are not as frequent as in Italian sources. And this is not only the case in the Easter tropes, but occurs in the Sanctus and Agnus Dei tropes to other feasts as well. Whereas, in the Aquitanian introductions we observed how the assembly was primarily present in the trope text as *singers* and *performers* of the chant, we may note that, in the Italian tradition, the assembly is more expressively present in the trope text as praying supplicants, calling upon the One who is praised by the angels, the Seraphim and the Cherubim, or the holy ones as in the *Pie Christe* quoted above.

This can be illustrated by the Sanctus trope *Quem Cherubim atque Seraphim* found in a number of Italian sources, here quoted from the Beneventan manuscript Ben 34:[50]

> *Sanctus,*
> Quem Cherubim atque Seraphim
> incessanter proclamant:
> *Sanctus*
> Qui senas alas habent
> quottidie decantant.
> *Sanctus dominus deus Sabaoth,*
> Pater prolique,
> flamineo almo,
> qui est ante saecula
> nunc et in aevum.
> *Pleni sunt caeli et terra gloria tua,*
> *Osanna in excelsis.*
> Cui pueri Hebreorum
> obviantes clamabant:
> *Benedictus qui venit in nomine domini.*
> Et plebs Hebrea
> vociferantes,
> vaticinantes dicebant:
> *Osanna in excelsis*

For the moment disregarding the strange form of the Latin, we see that it is a chant addressed to the Father, the Son and the Holy Spirit, *Pater (i e patri) prolique flamineo almo*. To these the Cherubim and Seraphim who have six wings, the young boys and people of Jerusalem bring their praises. A trope to the *Osanna in excelsis* found in Northern Italian sources, reads as follows:

> *Osanna*
> Agie, altissime domine,
> Adiuva, libera, salvifica, protege
> Quos creatos redemisti tuo sanguine.
> Paradisi gaudiis dona frui iugiter.
> Cherumbim coniungi coetibus valeant
> Seraphimque tibi dulce dant organa
> *In excelsis.*[51]

The text begins with an address formed in the vocative to the holy highest Lord: *agie, altissime domine.* In the next line, four imperatives implore the Lord to help and liberate the supplicants. The verbs are cumulated without any binding word, *adiuva, libera, salvifica, protege.* The object, *nos,* is not mentioned until the next line, where it refers to *quos redemisti tuo sanguine,* "those whom you redeemed with your blood". Then, there is a variant of the theme "give us eternal peace" which we have noted to be usual in the Agnus Dei as well, beseeching the Lord for the eternal joys of Paradise. Not until in the last two lines is the laudative theme of the *Osanna* introduced in the wish to join the Cherubim and the Seraphim in their praises. And here we also find phrases like the ones of the Prefaces mentioned above[52]. But here these phrases are used as trope texts:

> Cui Cherubim et Seraphim non cessant clamare dicentes . . .

As in the *Te Deum,* the praying assembly speaking in the trope texts "implores the One whom the angels glorify".

Te Deum

It seems as if the *Te Deum* has been a particularly important textual base for the Italian Sanctus tropes. Of course, this is natural enough since part of the Sanctus itself is a central part of the *Te Deum.* A significant number of phrases given in the *Te Deum* also occur as tropes to the Sanctus. So the laudative *tibi* clauses at the beginning of the hymn are, for instance, all used as trope texts. Again, the supplicative formulas at the end recall a tradition we have seen richly exemplified both in the Agnus Dei and in the Sanctus: "Therefore, we pray, help your servants, whom you have redeemed with your precious blood":

Te ergo quaesumus:
Tuis famulis subveni,
Quos pretioso sanguine redemisti

In Italian manuscript sources, the lines of the *Te Deum* given here in italics are also found as trope elements to the Sanctus, either in the same form as in the *Te Deum* or in a slightly different form. This indicates the importance of the hymn as the inspiration for the composition of trope texts in the Italian tradition:

Te Deum laudamus.
Te Dominum confitemur.
Te aeternum Patrem omnis terra veneratur.
Tibi omnes angeli,
Tibi caeli et universae potestates,
Tibi Cherubim et Seraphim incessabili voce proclamant:
Sanctus, Sanctus, Sanctus, Dominus Deus Sabaoth!
Pleni sunt caeli et terra maiestatis gloriae tuae!

Te gloriosus apostolorum chorus,
Te prophetarum laudabilis numerus,
Te martyrum candidatus laudat exercitus.
Te per orbem terrarum sancta confitetur Ecclesia
Patrem immensae maiestatis,
Venerandum tuum verum et unicum Filium,
Sanctum quoque paraclitum Spiritum.
Tu rex gloriae, Christe,
Tu Patris sempiternus es Filius.
Tu ad liberandum suscepturus hominem non horruisti virginis uterum.
Tu devicto mortis aculeo aperuisti credentibus regna caelorum.
Tu ad dexteram Dei sedes in gloria Patris.
Iudex crederis esse venturum.
Te ergo quaesumus:
Tuis famulis subveni,
Quos pretioso sanguine redemisti.
Aeterna fac cum sanctis tuis gloria numerari.
Salvum fac populum tuum, Domine.
Et benedic hereditati tuae
Et rege eos et extolle illos *usque in aeternum,*[53]

*

Considering the more or less distinctive traits in the Italian Agnus Dei tropes, it is tempting to enter into the discussion on the relationship between the Sicilian and Beneventan traditions. The two manuscripts Madrid 288 and Madrid 289 were both written in Palermo, as has been most recently shown by David Hiley. According to Hiley they both reflect a Normand tradition: "the two Palermo tropers . . . are likely to have been the result of the new recension carried out by a precentor (of the royal chapel?) who put his own individual stamp upon the repertories he knew from Normandy and from the Norman monasteries of Southern Italy."[54] On the relation between Benevento and Sicily he says: "It will have been noticed that none of the important sources from Benevento and Monte Cassino have appeared in the diagrams so far: *this is because the Sicilian books show almost no interesting material from that or from any other part of Italy"* (my italics).[55]

Both in the main structure of the Agnus Dei and in the trope texts these two manuscripts reflect a Northwestern Frankish repertory. Their Agnus Dei repertories are identical — with two exceptions: Ma 289 contains two Agnus Dei tropes which are not found in Ma 288, namely *Conditor polorum* and *Splendor patris*. One of them, *Conditor polorum,* is only found in the manuscript Ma 289. It differs in main structure as well as in its vocabulary from tropes to the Agnus Dei in the Northwestern tradition. The two tropes are placed at the very beginning of the fascicle of Agnus Dei tropes in the manuscript. The so called *lex Baumstark,*[56] which says that new items added to the liturgical repertory are regularly placed *before* the older items when inserted into the repertory in the manuscripts, supports the interpretation that these two tropes were new items added to the "old" Norman repertory retained in the manuscript Ma 289. At least the trope *Conditor polorum* might then prove to be an exception to the general rule observed by David Hiley and be an example of a text from the South Italian repertory being adopted into the Norman tradition kept in Sicily:

> Conditor polorum
> omniumque salvator,
> *Agnus dei, qui tollispeccata mundi, miserere nobis.*
> Tu redemisti nos
> sanguine tuo sacro.
> *Agnus dei, qui tollispeccata mundi, miserere nobis.*
> Gaudia supernae pacis
> dona nobis benigne.
> *Agnus, dei, qui tollis peccata mundi, miserere nobis.*
> Amen   (CT IV, 44)

The structure of this song, with the base liturgical text repeated in full phrases and given as a parallel to the trope elements, does not so much recall a Norman structure as an Italian one. Phrases like *tu redemisti nos sanguine tuo sacro,* "You redeemed us with Your holy blood" in the second trope element and the prayer of the last element, *Dona nobis . . . gaudia supernae pacis,* as well as the vocative *benigne* "Give us the joys of heavenly peace, o benign one", and finally the ending of the prayer by the word *Amen,* certainly remind us of the traits that we meet in the South Italian tropes, which do not occur in manucripts outside the Italian repertory. In Benevento, another trope, *Salus et vita,* has an additional element after *Supplicum preces/benigne exaudi/atque tuis/ miserere famulis:* also beginning with *Conditor* and ending with *Amen:*

> Conditor mundi,
> exaudi nos, clemens,
> et parce nobis
> regnans in aeternum.
> Amen.   (CT IV, 84)

All these indications suggest that *Conditor polorum* may be an example of a trope originating from South Italy and which has been included in the repertory of the trope manuscript Ma 289 by the composer in Palermo.[57]

CONCLUSION

In this study we have followed a few central themes developed in the tropes to the Agnus Dei and the Sanctus but also existant in tropes of other genres. We have seen how these tropes are primarily, in the Western tradition, formed as invocations functioning as theological expositions over the nature of divinity. In the trope texts, God is defined in relative clauses *(qui es, qui sedes,* etc), by verbs in the present participle form depicting the reigning King and Judge *(regens, sedens, residens, discutiens,* etc . . .) But most characteristic are the series of abstract nouns such as *pax, lux, sapientia;* these follow a long patristic tradition. We have noticed the central place of the trinitarian theme in repertories after the middle of the eleventh century especially in the Northwestern sources.

We have focused on the introductions in the Aquitanian tradition. These introductory trope elements have a double function. They tie the chant to the specific theme of the day, in the same way as is familiar from the proper tropes. They are invitations to sing. By words as *psallite, canite, dicite, voce praecelsa, una voce* etc the singers are exhorted to perform the chant in a loud unison voice. Finally we have seen tropes in the Italian traditions functioning as prayers to Christ as the sacrificed lamb "who redeemed us with His own blood," *qui redemisti nos sanguine tuo sacro.*

We have also observed how phrases and structures used in the trope texts recall other liturgical texts in the same tradition, such as the Litanies of the Saints, the Prefaces, the *Gloria in excelsis,* as well as the Mozarabic *Preces* and the *Te Deum* — particularly in the Italian tropes.

Of course, we have only touched on a few themes among many. Other studies remain to be done on other themes and on other trope genres — not to mention the sequences. In the future, when we have access to a concordance of the entire vocabulary of all the different trope genres, such studies will be made much easier.[58] Surely they will give us a deeper understanding of the rich treasure represented in these texts which reflects the spiritual life of the medieval mind in different expressions. In this work we need *pax et sapientia* . . .

Notes

1. Oxford, Bodl. Libr. MS 775, folios 72v, 74v; Cf. also Cambridge Corpus Christi College MS 473, folios 73v—74.

2. On the main structure of the Agnus Dei in different traditions see G. Iversen, *Corpus Troporum IV, Tropes de l'Agnus Dei, Edition critique suivie d'une étude analytique,* Acta Universitatis Stockholmiensis, Studia Latina Stockholmiensia XXVI, Stockholm 1980, 210—224 *et passim.* (Hereafter, Corpus Troporum = CT). Not only in analyzing the main structure of the troped chants but also in analyzing central themes in the tropes we discern different traditions. Thus, we speak of a Western tradition, divided into a Northwestern and a Southwestern, an Aguitanian tradition and of a tradition before and after 1050 respectively. We speak of an Eastern tradition and of Italian traditions — a North Italian, South Italian and Beneventan tradition. Then, there is the composite transitional tradition in the "zone de transition" to use the term introduced by Michel Huglo (NKLL Nordiskt kollokvium i latinsk liturgiforskning, Photocopied Reports, 3, Hanaholmen-Helsinki 1975). It also seems relevant to speak of a Catalonian/Pyrenean tradition after 1100 for instance. All these very roughly divided traditions can be further divided into smaller and more local traditions, many of which are worth studies of their own. It is important to note however, as has often been pointed out, that the boundaries between different geographical as well as chronological traditions are often very vague. In the same trope repertory we can find tropes of very different age and of different provenance side by side.

3. The text of the Gallican Litany in Paris, B.N.Lat.MS 13 159, folios 163—166. See G. Knopp, *Sanctorum nomina seriatim, Römische Quartalschrift für christliche Altertumskunde und Kirchengeschichte,* Bd 65, 3—4, 1970 184 ff; Cf.CT IV, 199.

4. *Gloria in excelsis* as basis for the Agnus Dei and its tropes cf. CT IV, 197—199; 253—259.

5. Madrid, B.N., MS 19421, f. 90v—91; Cf C. Blume, E. Bannister, *Analecta Hymnica Medii Aevi,* Bd 47, nr 271; The Sanctus texts quoted in this article are taken from the material for the critical edition of tropes to the Sanctus to be published by the author as a volume of the *Corpus Troporum.* References to the AH are indicating the number of the trope in AH 47.

6. AH 47, 124.

7. AH 45, p. 201.

8. Cf. G. Manz, *Ausdrucksformen der lateinischen Liturgiesprache bis ins elfte Jahrhundert,* Beuron, 1941, nr 561.

9. Walpole, A.E., *Early Latin Hymns,* Cambridge 1922, 35—39.

10. Migne, J.P., *Patrologiae cursus completus. Series Latina* (PL) *CXI, 20.*

11. PL CIXX, 266.

12. AH 50, 231.

13. Here quoted from R. de Gourmont, *Le latin mystique,* Paris, 1913, 118.

14. Karlheinz Schlager, *Zur musikalischen Gestalt und Überlieferung von "Trinitas, Unitas, Deitas",* Journal of the Plainsong & Medieval Music Society, Vol. 6, 1984, 8—14.
The text of *Trinitas, unitas, deitas* is analyzed by the author in *Music as Ancilla verbi and Words as Ancilla musicae;* On the interpretation of the Musical and Textual Form of the two Tropes to *Osanna in excelsis; Laudes deo and Trinitas, unitas, deitas,* Liturgische Tropen (Münchener Beiträge zur Mediävistik und Renaissance-Forschung 36) Hrsg. G. Silagi. München 1985; cf Dag Norberg, *L'accentuation des mots dans le vers latin du Moyen Age,* Kungl. Vitterhets Historie och Antikvitets Akademien, Filologiskt arkiv 32. Stockholm 1985, 59—60.

15. Paris, B.N.MS lat. 10508, fol. 134.

16. AH 53, nr 87.

17. PL CXXV, 542.

18. Schlager, op. cit.

19. PL CXXV, 575.

20. Cf. R. Jonsson, *Historia. Etudes sur la genèse des offices versifiés,* Acta universitatis Stock-holmiensis, Studia Latina Stockholmiensia XV, Stockholm 1968, 164—176; Although the texts for the office of the Holy Trinity had been prepared already by Alcuin, the Feast of the Holy Trinity was not universally declared a separate feast until 1334 by the pope John XXII. In England, however, this feast had been of great importance for a long time by then. Thomas Becket was consecrated bishop on the Holy Trinity feast in 1162 and, before that, there seems to have been a strong tradition in England and in the Northwest of the Frankish region of celebrating the Holy Trinity in a separate feast. Cf. *op.cit.* and F. Cabrol, *Le Culte de la Trinité dans la liturgie de la fête de la Trinité,* Ephemerides Liturgicae, 14 (1931), 270—278.; P. Brow, *Zur Geschichte der Dreifaltigkeitsfestes,* Archiv für Liturgiewissenschaft, 1 (1950), 65—81.

21. PL XIVC, 530; PL CI, 55—56.

22. Paris, B.N. MS lat. 10508, fol. 121—121v.

23. *Ibid.* fol. 118v—119; AH 47, nr 256.

24. Cf. CT IV, 225—228.

25. Cf. CT IV, 270—274.

26. Cf. CT IV, 96—97.

27. M. Huglo, *Antiphone antiche per la "fractio panis",* Ambrosius 31, 1955. 85—95.

28. Cf. CT IV, 272.

29. AH 47, nr 249.

30. Paris, B.N. MS lat. 1084, fol. 236.

31. L. Elfving, *Etude lexicographique sur les séquences limousines,* Acta Universitatis Stockholmiensis, Studia Latina Stockholmiensia VII, Stockholm 1962.

32. *Missale gallicanum vetus, Rerum ecclesiasticarum documenta,* Fontes III, ed. L.C. Mohlberg OSB, Rome 1958, 78.

33. *Ibid.,* 86.

34. It is a well-known observation that the tropes from the South Italian, the Beneventan, tradition, have been regarded for a long time a second- or third-class material, or even worse. To Clemens Blume, the obscure readings, the "bad" Latin, the structure and the arrangement of the tropes, were all rather disgusting. "Die Handschriften von Benevent sind in einem so trostlosen Zustande, dass wir von Mitteilung der Varianten absehen", Blume remarks for instance to the Beneventan version of the Gloria trope *Christus surrexit* with its interesting prosula added to the trope (AH 47, 222). Maybe the Beneventan tropes were left in peace for so long partly due to this attitude.

35. Among the interesting studies on the Italian material we can note L. Brunner's studies on the repertories of Nonantola: *The Sequences of Verona Bibl. Cap. CVII and the Italian Sequence Tradition.* (Diss.ined.), Univ. of North Carolina, Chapel Hill 1977. Editions of tropes to the Proper and to the Ordinary in the Beneventan manuscript sources are under preparation by John Boe and Alejandro Planchart in *Beneventanum Troporum Corpus.*

36. *CT IV, 221—224.*

37. Text from B. Opferman, *Litania Italica,* Ephemerides Liturgicae, 72, 1958, 310—319.

38. Cf. CT IV, 78—82, 88.

39. Text from E. Bischop, *The Litany of the Saints in the Stowe Missal, Liturgica Historia,* Oxford (1918) 1962, 142 ss. See also P. De Clerck, *La "Prière universelle" dans les liturgies latines,* Liturgiewissenschaftliche Quellen und Forschungen, Münster Westfahlen 1977, 275 ss.

40. D. Norberg, *Introduction á l'étude de la versification médiévale,* Acta Universitatis Stockholmiensis, Studia Latina Stockholmiensia V, Stockholm 1958, 78 and 97.

41. CT IV, 51—52; I am grateful to Professor Leo Treitler, who has generously helped me to analyse the different versions from a musicological point of view.

42. For a further analysis of the versions of the trope *Laudes deo,* see my article *Music as Ancilla verbi* . . . in which Professor Charles M. Atkinson has made the analysis of the melodies of the different versions of *Laudes deo;* AH 47, nr 340.

43. Cf. CT IV, 195 ss.

44. See W. Meyer, *Die Preces der Mozarabischen Liturgie,* Abhandlungen der Königlichen Gesellschaft der Wissenschaften zu Göttingen, Berlin 1907.
   Let us note that it is not exclusively in the Italian tropes that we can trace the Mozarabic *preces.* Also in Aquitanian tropes we can recognize similar formulas. Again it is possible to relate formulas in the trope texts to phrases used in other liturgical texts in the same tradition. The Agnus Dei trope *Miserere super nos* in Aquitania recalls the same sort of short formulaic phrases used in the *Preces* of the Spanish liturgy which are also found in Aquitanian graduals from the same period investigated by Michel Huglo in his article, *Les preces des Graduels aquitains empruntés à la liturgie hispanique,* Hispania sacra, 8 (1955), 361—383.

45. Meyer, *op.cit.,* 15;

46. Benevento, Bibl. cap. MS 40, fol. 26.

47. Benevento, Bibl. cap. MS 34, fol. 283.

48. Benevento, Bibl. cap. MS 35, fol. 196.

49. Monte Cassino, MS 546, fol. 67v and Roma, Bibl Apost. Vat. Urb. 602, fol. 62.

50. Ben 34, fol. 282v.

51. Here taken from the ms Padua, Bibl. cap. MS 47, fol. 1.

52. Cf. p. 39s. above.

53. An investigation of the relation between the formulas of the *Te Deum* and the tropes particulary in the Italian repertories is evidently promising to be fruitful. Such a study is still waiting to be done.

54. David Hiley, *The Norman Chant Traditions — Normandy, Britain, Sicily,* Proceedings of the Royal Musical Association, vol. 107 (1980—81), p. 8.

55. *Ibid.,* p. 5.

56. A. Baumstark, *Das Gesetz der Erhaltung des Alten in liturgisch hochwertiger Zeit,* Jahrbuch für Liturgiewissenschaft, 7 (1927) 1—23; Cf. Niels K. Rasmussen, *Liturgie de l'église particulière et liturgie de l'église universelle,* Unité et diversité des Pontificaux Latins aux VIIIe, IXe et Xe siècles, Conférences Saint-Serge 1975, Rome 1976, 393—410, p. 406.

57. Cf. D. Hiley, *Quanto c'è di Normanno nei tropari Siculo-Normanni?.* Rivista Italiana di musicologia, XVIII, 1983, 12.

58. By means of computer concordances are made of the entire vocabulary of the material included in the Corpus Troporum volumes. These concordances can be consulted at the Corpus Troporum office, Institutionen för klassiska språk, Stockholms Universitet, S-106 91 Stockholm, SWEDEN.

Ritva Jacobsson and Leo Treitler

Tropes and the Concept of Genre

I

"What is a trope?"

Why do we ask this question repeatedly? What sorts of answers do we seek? It is first of all a practical question, one that has to be asked by the editors of such publications as the *Analecta Hymnica* and the *Corpus Troporum,* and answered with every decision about the inclusion of one text in those editions and the exclusion of another.

But throughout its history it has had more attention as a scientific question. What did the compilers of manuscripts around the turn of the Millenium intend when they wrote "Tropus" at the head of a text? What is the origin of "the trope"? What is "its" history? The last two questions presuppose some idea about what the "it" is. What is it, about whose origins we have been asking? What can we identify as the subject of the continuous history that we would like to trace? The question "what is a trope?" has most often been raised explicitly in connection with questions about origins and history, and that connection has determined a great deal about the kinds of answers that have been entertained. It presupposes a multitude of works with a constellation of shared features that is more or less consistently associated with the name "trope", and whose appearance in a succession of such items constitutes the basis of continuity in the category bearing that name. An answer to the question, then, is given by describing that constellation of features. But that has been difficult, as we shall be reminded in a moment.

None of the scientific questions can be answered without at the same time addressing — at least tacitly — similar questions about types of liturgical song known by other names: sequence, hymn, versus, prosa, prosula, laudes . . . To ask "what is a trope?" is to ask "in what sorts of partitions does the world of medieval ecclesiastical song present itself to us?"

There is a third sense of the question, that we might identify as the aesthetic, or critical sense. It is raised implicitly whenever we engage a single trope with the intention of judging its qualities and values. We can do that only if we have a sense of the norms and standards for the making of such things. This is no more than to say that we cannot judge the meaning of a thing without having some idea about the kind of thing that it is. Without entering into the never-ending controversy about whether understanding about norms and standards is essential to the criticism of art as a general rule, we can be certain that a single trope text with its melodic setting does not carry with it — at least not for us, in the present state of our experience — a sufficient artistic universe to enable us to understand it.

In all three senses — the practical, the historical, and the aesthetic — the question asks for the definition of a "genre", a word we commonly use to designate the classes, clusters, or kinds of art works that we study. We use the word easily in speaking of the categories of art works, and it has then a neutral connotation, doing little more than identifying the divisions in a taxonomy. But the concept of "genre" can function more actively and productively in the analysis of art and its history, and that potential rests on its multi-dimensionality. It brings together perspectives on the artist, on the work, and on the public. With respect to the artist, a genre represents a tradition of making that sets tasks and transmits conventions and models in relation to which the artist exercises his own intentions. This perspective focuses more on practice than on products. With focus on the work, a genre represents a complex of structural and stylistic features and features of content. It is the basis for a classification of the morphologies of works. With focus on the public, a genre represents the function or purpose of a kind of art work, addressed to a particular public, and the expectations and responses of the public in the light of that function and of the artistic means that are adapted to it. Those means will include not only morphological features and content, but matters of tone and attitudes as well. To take the most obvious sort of case, in the genres of spy or mystery novels, both the details of formal conventions and subject matter on one side, and tone on the other, are understood in relation to the objective of delivering both intellectual stimulation and the experience of terror to readers.

Despite the separate identification of these perspectives in this description, it is only in their interaction that the genre concept can produce understanding of individual works.

But even in investigating the history of a genre, we require such a multidimensional approach. In biology the development of evolutionary theory — that is, of a theory about the history of species — depended on the replacement of purely morphological species identification with classification involving the interaction of genetics, morphology, and ecology. Similarly, if the classification of medieval ecclesiastical song is to serve as a basis for the understanding of the history of its genres, it will have to be a classification based not only on the morphology of individual songs, but on the interaction of that factor with the generation and transmission of songs and with their function vis-a-vis a public.

The genre concept has been in use since classical times — then with its companion concept, propriety or *decorum*. The latter stood for the idea that particular conventions, which could be spelled out in the form of rules, were appropriate to particular genres in the light of their objectives or functions.

In view of their functions, genres develop norms and conventions of theme and manner which are available to artists working in the genre, and which are already intelligible to audiences, who in turn develop conventionalized responses to them. Conventions on both sides undergo development through their interaction within the tradition of the genre, and it is to these that one has paid attention in tracing the history of the genre.

Artists working in a genre are conscious of a tradition; they imitate, parody, transform what their predecessors have done. They work to carry forward a standard that constitutes the core of the genre. Such is the historical aspect of the "genre" concept from the viewpoint of the artist. If we do not have that aspect in mind, it is misleading to speak of genres at all. "Genre" is more than a concept for building a taxonomy of art works. One question we shall have to consider is how the genre concept can serve to elucidate the history of tropes.

A shift of emphasis has taken place in the use of the genre concept more recently. It is a shift toward the point of view of the beholder, and its core idea is the notion of art as an exchange, or transaction. The interest is in the role of genre as a system of norms to which works may be related, a code by virtue of which they become intelligible, coherent, and meaningful. The conventions of genre make the conveyance of meaning possible by providing categories in which to register the things encountered. An account of genres would be an attempt to define the classes which have been functional in the processes of making and understanding art works, the sets of premises and expectations that have enabled publics to relate art works to their own worlds. Genre, from this point of view as well, is not simply a taxonomic class. It is the basis for an understanding of art works as aesthetic objects, for the critic today, as well as for the beholder in history.

A further question we shall have to consider, then, is how the genre concept can contribute to a critical understanding of tropes.

These considerations about the genre concept reflect mainly the experience of the history and criticism of art and literature. But still "genre" has something, if not everything, to do with taxonomy. It will be well, therefore, to think also about what we expect when we think of tropes as a genre from the point of view of classification in theory. By inference, we will thereby be considering what might have been intended by those who wrote "tropus" at the head of a text in a medieval manuscript.

The heuristic value of systems of classification depends on the premise that we can partition the collections of things we are classifying so that everything falls into one class or other. It is only then that our classifications have theoretical or explanatory impact. To take a general example from the field of chant study, in identifying a melody as "plagal" we are saying two sorts of things about it. For one, we encode certain of its features that have to do with the relation of its range to its tonic; we describe its morphology. For the other we relate it to a classification scheme that partitions the collection of all chants and in doing so we make a theoretical and explanatory claim about the tone system that underlies them. That is, when we say the melody is "plagal" we are not merely labelling or indexing it for convenience; we are making a claim about how it works and how it relates to the system. And that claim is an important aspect of what we want to say about the melody.

By contrast, the classification of books by librarians and fingerprints by policemen are acts of indexing for purposes of identification, storage, and retrieval. The grading systems for eggs and meat are ways of distinguishing size or quality, and cost. The ranking systems for military and civil service employees signify different levels of experience, ability, responsibility, authority, and salary. All such classifications schemes serve some practical purpose of identification and have no theoretical impact. They may in fact partition the entire universe of items that they classify, but that fact is not pertinent for the information that they are mainly intended to convey.

A consequence of this difference between heuristic and utilitarian classification, as we may call them, is that the former amounts to a kind of concept formation, whereas the latter does not. We place something under a certain class and group it with other things under the same class because of certain characteristics that we regard as essential to the object and the class. Those characteristics really give us the *concept* of that class. There is a concept that represents the characteristics possessed by chants that we classify as "plagal", the *plagal* concept. In identifying a chant as "plagal", we place it under that concept, and thereby we make a substantial claim about its nature. On the other hand when we label a book with the designation "ML 410" our primary interest is not usually in the concept of that class ("music literature, biographical").

To come to our own subject, when we say that a liturgical song is a trope or sequence or hymn, unless that represents some specific filing or indexing decision, we are implicitly making a claim about the way the whole system of medieval ecclesiastical song worked and why one sort was different from another. There must be an implication that we control — or at least that we aim to control — the concept of each of those classes and the relationships among the several concepts. What we aim for in making classifications is systematic understanding. We aim to se how the characteristics which qualify a thing as a member of a class, are related to other clusters of characteristics. The more we can see of that, the more we can feel that we understand the organization of the world we are studying — the more, to quote Plato, we can feel we are "carving nature by the joints". [1]On the other hand, the further away we remain from that objective, the more the act of classifying will be a compulsive but futile exercise.

In our classfication of ecclesiastical song the more we can identify and distinguish clusters of characteristics having to do with form, stylistic features of language and melody, length, ritual function, subject matter, tone, etc., the more we will have the sense that we understand how the systems of medieval song work. The further away we remain from that objective, the more we should wonder whether the names we use really represent classes, and whether the material we are looking at really bears that sort of systematic analysis. Then we will still be left with the question, what did the compilers of medieval ecclesiastical books mean to convey when they wrote "tropus" above an item? What does it mean that Notker called his collection of sequences "Liber hymnorum", when we think that we know the difference between a hymn and a sequence? Was the word of medieval song partitioned in the way that we expect our worlds to be partitioned when we attach names to the things that we find in them?

Having reviewed in the abstract what can be implied in calling a song "trope", we now turn to the concrete material of tropes to inquire whether and how it may be productive to regard them from the point of view of "genre".

It seems from this review that we are unlikely to achieve, as a matrix for a trope genre, a classification of medieval ecclesiastical song that is systematic in a very high degree. For we have seen how differently the factors of form, content, and function can interact at the level of the individual song. And as they do not follow consistent patterns of interaction from song to song, they do not produce sharply defined categories at higher levels of classification. As a consequence of this situation the efforts to partition the material neatly show that any such scheme must be so multidimensional that the goal of "carving nature by the joints" will necessarily elude it. It would entail a very large number of classes, most of them with very few members, and with uncertain lines of demarcation between them. What is more, in the medieval sources there is not only a degree of inconsistency in the classes to which individual items are assigned, there is an inconsistency about the criteria for establishing classes altogether: "versus", which simply means "a collection of lines", and may be assigned to various styles and functions; "laudes", which speaks to a kind of function or tone; "prosa" or "prosula", which suggest certain morphological characteristics.

Jorge Luis Borges wrote about a certain Chinese encyclopedia in which are identified the following classes of animals: belonging to the emperor, embalmed, tame, sucking pigs, sirens, fabulous, stray dogs, included in the present classification, frenzied, innumerable, drawn with a very fine camel-hair brush, et cetera, having just broken the water pitcher, that from a long way off look like flies. [2] We could read this as a parody, exaggerated only in degree but not in kind, of the classification of medieval song that is implied by the naming behaviour of medieval manuscripts (and, by the way, of medieval lists and classifications of all sorts of things). What is the matter with it? It poses categories that do not strike contrasts with respect to consistent sets of dimensions; they cannot therefore be compared, and one cannot decide whether a thing belongs to one category or another. It is unsystematic, and it cannot provide a very good basis for theoretical understanding. But instead of regarding this sort of thing as a primitive trait in the medieval intellect, we might consider that our expectations in naming and classifying are inappropriate to the early medieval way of organizing material, and look for alternatives that may bring us closer. We can suggest two intersecting ways of thinking about the problem that may provide better access.

For the first, this exercise in inquiring "What's in a name?" has amounted to a sort of re-enactment of Ludwig Wittgenstein's reasoning about the way we think about categories and whether particulars belong to them. [3] His question is about how we decide that particular activities are called "games".

> I mean board-games, card-games, ball-games, Olympic games, and so on. What is common to them all? — Don't say: "There *must* be something common, or they would not be called 'games'" — but *look and see* whether there is something that is common to all. — For if you look at them you will not see something that is common to *all,* but similarities, relationships, and a whole series of them at that . . .
>
> And the result of this examination is: we see a complicated network of similarities, sometimes similarities of detail.
>
> I can think of no better expression to characterize these similarities than "family resemblances;" for the various resemblances between members of a family; build, features, colour of eyes, girth, temperament, etc. etc., overlap and criss-cross in the same way.
>
> . . . And we extend our concept as in spinning a thread we twist fibre on fibre. And the strength of the thread does not reside in the fact that some one fibre runs through its whole length, but in the overlapping of many fibres.

We regard this piece as a trope, and another because it is in some important ways like the first, and then another and another, and so on. But in the collection that we accumulate in that way there can be two that are very *unlike* one another. Does it not seem likely that, to the medieval mind, the category "tropus" formed itself in just this way? There are different aspects of tropes in respect of which they may be alike or dissimilar from one to another: the proximity to the mass, the assimilation and juxtaposition of biblical and other texts, the use of certain stereotyped texts, such as the exchange at the sepulchre, the exhortation to sing, the identification of feasts, the apostrophizing of a group of celebrants, the modelling on antiphons, hymns, or other types of liturgical song, the tone of praise, the practice of concretizing pre-existant texts as speech-acts. If these are the fibres in the thread that runs through the trope genre, then some of them are longer than others. But the thread itself is constituted by the overlapping and interweaving and criss-crossing of the fibres. We have only to add to Wittgenstein's image that any of these fibres may run into another thread in what is really a network.

It is striking that we cannot arrive at a very satisfactory characterization of the trope genre by means of the identification of a constellation of features that is common to tropes, that is by way of the morphological description of works.

Putting this in the terms of our earlier discussion of the genre concept, it means that of the three perspectives that this concept entails, the view on tropes from the perspective of the work has not been very productive. Our observations and generalizations have been focused instead on the other two points of the triangle, as we might put it, the maker and the public. We have been led to interpret the material in terms of systems and traditions for composing tropes — in the literal sense of putting them together — adapted to particular ritual functions and purposes, cast in particular tones, directed at particular celebrants. The generative systems for tropes have certain points of contact with systems for composing other kinds of ecclesiastical songs, and the several systems jointly constitute a larger planetary system that is dependent upon the central function of the mass, itself a fluctuating phenomenon. The individual items that were produced and that we find depicted in the manuscripts, always in different local configurations, are better understood in the context of such a total dynamic system, than in terms of a sharply partitioned classification of fixed works.

That brings us to the second way of thinking about the problem. What we have just said amounts to a recognition that we are dealing with the productions of a culture that retained the residual habits and techniques of an oral tradition while exercising the technology of writing of which it was coming into increasing possession and control and which, conversely, was coming increasingly to control its productions. The fixed work is not the principal unit or the highest goal of artistic production in such a culture. Artistic production depends, not on a tradition of artists consciously working in view of an advancing standard to produce monuments of high art, but on generative systems through which the items of art that are needed may be produced locally, for local use, according to local needs. This is not to deny that artistic skill may be exercised and that productions of high aesthetic achievement may result. It is, however, to affirm that one of the premises on which the genre concept has been postulated — the centrality of the work and of a continuous tradition of works — is foreign to the culture with which we are dealing, and that the difficulties that have arisen in attempting to apply that concept here are directly related to that fact. These difficulties do not constitute a failure, but an important historical realization.

Some of the most characteristic features of the products of fully and residually oral traditions can be recognized among the tropes, and we have already taken note of them: expressions which are stereotyped, heavily patterned or formulaic, and highly contextualized; a rhapsodic manner of composition in which elements of different origins are juxtaposed and recombined; highly evocative and referential language; the maker adopting the tone of the performer or speaker and addressing his *listeners* directly (thus the heavy use of the imperative and the second person plural).[4]

But on the other hand the material of the tropes shows, perhaps better than any other similar material, how the technology of writing in the early centuries of its widespread use, was in the service of this kind of artistic production. The core of the *Quem quaeritis* tradition is a *text,* the bases of many early trope compositions are biblical texts, the practice of juxtaposing texts, especially with such a large number of texts in circulation, was surely dependent on writing, the growing tendency to compose decorative — particularly hexameter — trope texts, and especially the close musical settings of these, must have been supported by writing.

These latter tendencies, in both poetry and music, begin to give to tropes the appearance of the pursuit of particular artistic tasks under particular artistic standards. In this sense the tropes took on a characteristic that has generally been taken as a basis for the identification of a genre. So that perhaps we may say that it is an aspect of the history of the trope genre, that it took on one of the main attributes of a genre in the course of its history. While it seems not justifiable to assume the applicability of the genre concept to early medieval song from the start, it may be that the changes that were taking place during the Middle Ages can in part be characterized by observing that the Genre concept *becomes* relevant.

II

One of the most intriguing problems of medieval studies is that of the origin of medieval drama and hence of the birth of modern theatre. The question about the "trope" genre lies at the heart of that problem. But the material basis for the question seems to be simple and straightforward.

The liturgical Easter play always has just one little text, a dialogue between the women at the empty grave and the angel, always with the same three utterances: first a question, *Quem quaeritis in sepulchro, christicolae* — then the answer: *Iesum Nazarenum crucifixum, o caelicolae* and finally the response that changes everything: *Non est hic — surrexit sicut praedixerat* followed by the exhortation *Ite nuntiate quia surrexit, alleluia.*

This text appears in several sorts of liturgical books: missals, breviaries, antiphoners, tropers, etc. and it can be embodied in different series of antiphons, of tropes and of sequences, and in a sometimes highly elaborated liturgical play. It can be followed by the Resurrection introit, *Resurrexi et adhuc tecum sum,* and is then a trope, belonging to the mass; it can be followed by *Te deum,* which fits it for Matins, and it can be followed by various other songs. This has created the occasion for an enormous amount of writings. One principal task is to determine systems and categories in which to place the different *Quem quaeritis*-songs; another principal task, related to the first one, is to find out how the tradition began, what came first ... And then come all the problems of performance, of variants ... [5]

However, what is striking is that it is always the same small text that is transmitted, the three utterances with scarcely any changes, from the early tenth century down to Renaissance. Even embodied in a sophisticated context, with elaborated strophes in different meters, our text nucleus is always the same.

It is quite clear that this text was sung as a trope, is named trope in the rubrics of several manuscripts, just as it is true that in many other manuscripts it clearly is regarded as something other than a trope — for instance in those liturgical books not containing other tropes.

Now we will not deal at all with the liturgical drama-question, whether or not the drama originated as a trope. But there are at least two important conclusions from what we have said about *Quem quaeritis* for our subject: 1) We have an extremely clear case of a text being used *both* as a trope and as something else. 2) We have here the evidence of a dramatic genre of trope which has even been a model for other similar tropes constructed in the same way with a question, replies and an exhortation: *Quem quaeritis in praesepe* for Christmas, *Quem creditis ascendentem in caelum* for Ascension etc. [6]

But it can be said that the *Quem quaeritis* is a special type of trope, different from the normal trope. What then is a normal type of trope?

Instead of pursuing the long story of the attempts to define "trope" — let us quote the well-known definition by Durandus de Mende (1230—96).[7]

> Tropus est quidam versiculus qui praecipuis festivitatibus cantatur immediate ante introitum quasi quoddam praeambulum et continuatio ipsius introitus ut verbi gratia in festo Nativitatis. Continet autem tria tropus, videlicet antiphonam, versus et gloriam. (Rationale IV, cap. 5 § 5.).
>
> /The Trope is a kind of a little verse which on special feast days is sung immediately before the introit as a sort of a prelude and continuation of the very introit, for instance in the Christmas feast. The trope thus includes three items, that is the antiphon, the verses and the Gloria./

Hence, trope texts introduce and are intercalated in the mass songs. In order to learn what the normal case is for this genre, let us look at one or two examples, chosen from the rather rich tropers of Apt. These two manuscripts are the subject for a thorough study by Gunilla Björkvall, soon to be published. [8]

For now we will deal with the proper tropes. First, let us see how the later of the two, Apt 17, from the end of the 11th century, presents the tropes for the resurrection introit. It offers a rich choice, 13 sets of tropes. [9]

Example 1

Apt 17 (Resurr intr)

p126 11
    Hora est psallite
1.   iubet domnus canere
    eia dicite

» An(gelus) «
Quem quaeritis in sepulcro o xpisticole

» R(espondent) «
Hiesum nazarenum crucifixum o caelicole

» Ang(elus) «
Non est hic
surrexit sicut prędixerat
ite nunciate quia surrexit

» Cant(ores) «
Alleluia
ad sepulcrum residens angelus nunciat
resurrexisse Xpistum

» Ang(elus) «
Ecce completum est illud
quod olim ipse per prophetam dixerat
ad patrem taliter inquiens
RESUR(REXI ET ADHUC TECUM SUM . . .)

» Tr «
2.   Ecce pater cunctis ut iusserat ordo peractis
p127 RES(URREXI ET ADHUC TECUM SUM)
Victor ut ad caelos calcata morte redirem
POSU(ISTI SUPER ME MANUM TUAM)
Quo genus humanum pulsis erroribus altum
scanderet ad caelum teneo de morte triumphum
MIRABI(LIS FACTA EST SCIENTIA TUA)

» P «
DOMINE PRO(BASTI ME ET COGNOVISTI ME
TU COGNOVISTI SESSIONEM MEAM ET RESURRECTIONEM
MEAM)

» Al «
3.   Factus homo tua iussa pater moriendo peregi
RES(URREXI ET ADHUC TECUM SUM)
Abstuleras miserate manens mihi reddita lux est
POS(UISTI SUPER ME MANUM TUAM)
Plebs caecata meum nomen non novit amandum
MIRAB(ILIS FACTA EST SCIENTIA TUA)

» It tropos «
4.   Aurea lux remeat Hiesus iam morte perempta
sic cruciger patri Davidis fatur in odis
RESUR(REXI ET ADHUC TECUM SUM)

p128 Quo compos hominis caelos iam victor adirem
POS(UISTI SUPER ME MANUM TUAM)
Omne quod est fuerat superest tu noscis ob idque
MIR(ABILIS FACTA EST SCIENTIA TUA)
O paradisicole cherubin in laude ciete
ALLELUIA

» P « INTELLE(XISTI COGITATIONES MEAS A LONGE
SEMITAM MEAM ET DIRECTIONEM MEAM INVESTIGASTI)

» It(em) «

5. Ego autem constitutus sum rex
prędicans pręceptum tuum
et morte devicta
RES(URREXI ET ADHUC TECUM SUM)
Dormivi pater et surrexi diluculo
et somnus meus dulcis est mihi
POS(UISTI SUPER ME MANUM TUAM)
Ita pater sic placuit ante te
ut moriendo mortis mors fuissem
morsus inferni et mundi vita
MIR(ABILIS FACTA EST SCIENTIA TUA)
Qui abscondisti hec sapientibus
p129 et revelasti parvulis alleluia
ALLELUIA

» Ad gloria «
Sit semper illi gloria laus et honor
nos quaesumus conserves
in haec sacra solemnia canentes
eia eia
GLORIA SECULOR(UM) AMEN

» It tro «

6. En ego verus sol occasum meum novi
et super eum solus ascendens
RES(URREXI ET ADHUC TECUM SUM)
Destructo mortis imperio
POSU(ISTI SUPER ME MANUM TUAM)
Quoniam mors mea facta est mundi vita
MIR(ABILIS FACTA EST SCIENTIA TUA)
Exurge gloria mea fili
exurgam diluculo pater
ALLELUIA

» It(em) «

7.   Iam tua iussa pater mortem superando peregi
      RES(URREXI ET ADHUC TECUM SUM)

P130 Vincere quo mundum mortem zabuloque valere
      POSU(ISTI SUPER ME MANUM TUAM)
      Mistica perdocui gemina sacramenta sophię
      MIRA(BILIS FACTA EST SCIENTIA TUA)
      Omnia quae sperant pater hinc te laude canendo
      ALLELUIA
      EXPUR(GATE)

8.   Resurrexit dominus
      auctor lucis adest cui
      non pepercit pater inde
      refert illi gratias
      RES(URREXI)
      Passus ut homo
      surrexit ut deus
      ultro sustulit mortem
      qui omnibus dat vitam
      et nunc conlaudans patrem dicit
      ET ADHUC (TECUM SUM)
      Quo tremuit terra moriente
      quo pavefactus inferus ad se intrante

p131 nunc resurgens affatur patrem
      POS(UISTI SUPER ME MANUM TUAM)
      Corpus iacens in sepulcro
      munitur custodibus
      anima secum reduxit
      quos tenebat Tartarus
      fideles tantum
      MIR(ABILIS FACTA EST SCIENTIA TUA)
      Alleuia decantemus
      resurgenti domino
      omnis clerus atque vulgus
      cum fideli populo
      quem laus decet honor virtus
      in excelso solio
      ALLELUIA

      » P « SURREXIT

      » It tro «

9.   Gaudete et lętamini fratres
      quia surrexit dominus alleluia
      iocundemur cum illo dicentes eia

70

RES(URREXI)
Dum resurgeret in iudicio deus
p132 ET AD(HUC TECUM SUM)
Terremotus factus est magnus
angelus domini descendit de caelo
POS(UISTI SUPER ME MANUM TUAM)
Contremuit terra Xpisto surgente a mortuis
MIRAB(ILIS FACTA EST)
Custodes velut mortui effecti sunt
SCIENTIA (TUA)
Nimio timore angeli
ALLELUIA

10. Claustra destruxi inferni
et subverti potentias diaboli
RES(URREXI ET ADHUC TECUM SUM)
Te pater omne pariter proclamans conlaudat
POSU(ISTI SUPER ME MANUM TUAM)
Tu me probasti et cognovisti resurrectionem meam
tu me formasti
et manu dextera tua tenuit me
MIR(ABILIS FACTA EST SCIENTIA TUA)

11. Hodie resurrexit leo fortis
xpistus filius dei
p133 deo gratias dicite eia
RES(URREXI ET ADHUC TECUM SUM)
Gaudeamus omnes
resurrexit dominus
POS(UISTI SUPER ME MANUM TUAM)
Vicit leo de tribu Iuda
radix Iesse
MIR(ABILIS FACTA EST SCIENTIA TUA)

» It(em) «

12. Hunc diem Xpistus patri sacravit sic dicens
RES(URREXI ET ADHUC TECUM SUM)
Deus enim et homo pariter ego sum
POS(UISTI SUPER ME MANUM TUAM)
Ego dormivi somnumque cepi et ecce
MIR(ABILIS FACTA EST SCIENTIA TUA)
Leo fortis de sepulcro resurrexit hodie
deo gratias dicite eia
RES(URREXI ET ADHUC TECUM SUM)

13. Calcato mortis aculeo resurrexi hodie
eia eia

POSU(ISTI SUPER ME MANUM TUAM)
Quos redemit suo sacro sanguine
et vocavit ad gloriam
MIR(ABILIS FACTA EST SCIENTIA TUA)

The first set is the Easter dialogue, the old and famous *Quem quaeritis* about which we already have spoken. This dialogue has an equally old introduction, *Hora est psallite,* which also functions as an introduction in several other contexts. It is really an invitation to sing, without any allusions to the Christian context: "It is time, sing. The master (the bishop or priest) bids us sing. Say eia. "And after the dialogue, first the singers relay the angel's report that Christ is risen, then the angel passes from the dialogue to the introit antiphon: "It is fulfilled, that which he once said to the father through the prophet, saying thus: *Resurrexi."* The very special and typical function of the trope could not be better exemplified than by this trope line: introducing a sentence by explaining who says what, and to whom, binding together the Old Testament text with that of the gospel. Note the role of the adverbial expressions: *olim* — once upon a time, which places the text of the introit in its original context, and *taliter,* "thus", placing it now in its new context.

Following this first trope set, there are twelve more. Of these the 2nd, 3rd, 4th and 7th are hexameters of the "normal kind" — the introit is introduced and twice intercalated with one or two hexameters and eventually followed by one before the alleluia. In these texts it is mostly Jesus who speaks, in the first person, and the pronoun *ego* is even used more than once. Base liturgical text and trope text fit together syntactically. We can see how similar those hexameters in the different tropes are:

> Ecce *pater* cunctis ut *iusserat* ordo *peractis* (2)
> Factus homo tua *iussa pater* moriendo *peregi* (3)
> Iam tua *iussa pater* mortem superando *peregi* (7)

The father is apostrophized, the son has fulfilled *(peregi)* his orders *(iussa).* One could go on and look at many such small building blocks used repeatedly in slightly changed combinations. One sees also how the base liturgical text is paraphrased and explained, thus the somewhat obscure Psalm text *Mirabilis facta est scientia tua* has introductory tropes such as *Plebs caecata meum nomen non novit amandum* or *Omne quod est fuerat superest tu noscis ob idque* — the verb *nosco, novi* takes up *scientia.*

The fifth and sixth trope sets are different: they are in prose and have different themes or images. But they too begin by putting the introit text in the mouth of Christ risen, and this is very strongly underlined by the word *ego.* If we look more closely, we will find that the prosaic building blocks in these trope lines already belong to the Liturgy: scriptural quotations, echos from antiphons and responsories etc.

When we come to the ninth trope set, we can observe a quite different type. All the foregoing tropes are explanations, theological commentaries or ornamentations. Only the trope elements introducing the doxology, in the fifth trope set, and "Alleluia" in the eighth trope set have the classical hortatory form: *Sit semper illi gloria laus et honor . . . in haec sacra solemnia canentes,* and *Alleluia decantemus resurgenti . . .* which binds the jubilation to the actual feast.

But the ninth trope set begins by inviting the people to sing, and its form is very "classical": *Gaudete,* an exhortation in the imperative plural, directed to the singers *(fratres); quia,* which tells why; *iocondemur,* with its first-person subjunctive form, embraces the entire celebrating community. The connection with the introit text occurs through *cum illo* — it is Christ who says *Resurrexi.* This is the first occurrence of the word "eia" in all the tropes for this feast, except for the very beginning. The model for this procedure — an exhortation in the second person imperative, immediately followed by a subjunctive in the first person plural — is the Invitatory Psalm (95), *"Venite, adoremus."* This, being sung daily, was not only well known, but the rhythm of its procedure must have been assimilated deeply in the minds of all present. In this sense the "form" is a productive model, a mental template. [10]

Let us look at the rest of this trope: mere scriptural quotations, and half of them from the New Testament. The base liturgical text is cut into smaller pieces and its syntax is interrupted by the tropes:

	Trope		*Base text*
1	The earth was shaken when Christ rose from the dead	a	It was made wonderful
2	The guards became as though dead	b	through thy knowledge
3	and through the great fear caused by the angel		

The original order of the base text: a b

The order of the troped text: 1 a 2 b 3

The fact is that introit and trope do not fit together in a very obvious way.

In nos. 10—13 we have four trope sets to *Resurrexi* (or two, if we take the texts preceding and following the rubric "item" as belonging to the same set). Three types of trope expression are involved: In the first, the psalm is transformed to have Christ speak and introduce the word *Resurrexi.* In the second, quotations from other parts of the Bible are brought into this context (e.g. *leo fortis* from the Apocalypse). And in the third, the feast itself is named *(Hunc diem, hodie, gaudeamus, eia)*.

Apt 17 is not only a late manuscript, a very rich troper which represents different influences, but it is also a troper composed by someone who worked in a quite conscious manner, reworking, arranging. We can see how much he changed the set *Resurrexit dominus* which is transmitted with bad Latin in other sources. It is also very clear what is meant by ''trope'' here. The rubrics, the arrangement, show that the Apt scribe knew quite well what he meant by ''trope''.[10 bis].

Looking at the collection as a whole, it seems to be ordered on more than one principle. It begins with the old dramatized *Quem quaeritis* trope to the introit and the mass, perhaps because it had the greatest prestige. Then come three hexameter tropes of a similar type, presumably later than the first. The eighth seems much older, and could be introduced into this fine troper only after a thorough reworking. 9—13 seem to represent the oldest layer.

In any case, what is most interesting is that the Easter introit tropes in this book constitutes such a cross-section of genres. We shall return to this later. Now we may consider the introit tropes for Easter in Apt 18, the older of the two. The series begins also with *Quem quaeritis* and its introduction, which is followed by about half of the tropes in Apt 17, but presented *in nearly reverse order*. Using the numbering in Apt 17, they are 11—13, 9, some of 6, and finally 4 (the only hexameter trope in this series). This seems to substantiate the common understanding that the oldest tropes were of a more biblical type and were based on the poetic conceit of the invitation to the singer to perform the liturgical chant. In the later tropes, which are often in hexameters, the texts are more given over to commentary and ornamentation. [11] But we must consider the rest of the Proper tropes for Easter Sunday in the Apt manuscripts. The example is from Apt 18 (example 2).

Example 2

Apt 18 (Resurr off; com)

22

f41 » Ad of «
f41 v Iam surrexit dominus salvator mundi
       hodie apparuit mundo Christus Iesus
       cantate illi
       TERRA TREMUIT (ET QUIEVIT)
       Ab increpacione et ira furoris domini
       TERRA TREMUIT (ET QUIEVIT)
       Monumenta aperta sunt
       et multa corpora sanctorum surrexerunt
       DUM RESURGERE(T)
       Christus iudicaturus est vivos et mortuos

quando venerit
IN IUDICIO (DEUS)
(C)hristo resurgente a mortuis
venite adoremus eum omnes
huna voce proclamantes
ALLELUIA
Notus es dominus in Iudea
salus eterne
gracias agamus deo ipsi
eia et eia

» V « NOTUS IN IUDEA DEUS (IN ISRAEL MAGNUM NOMEN
EIUS)

f42   Factus est in pace locus eius
resurrexit dominus
gloria laus et honor sit semper illi eia
ET FACTUS EST IN PACE (LOCUS EIUS ET HABITATIO EIUS IN
SION)
Ibi confregit potencias
arcum et bellum fortissimum
IBI CONFREGIT CORNU ARCUM (SCUTUM ET GLADIUM ET
BELLUM
ILLUMINANS TU MIRABILITER A MONTIBUS AETERNIS)

» Ad comm «
(Venite populi ad sacrum . . .)
Laus honor virtus deo nostro
decus et imperium regi nostro
qui precium redemcionis nostre
» co « PASCHA NOSTRUM (IMMOLATUS EST CHRISTUS)
Peccata nostra ipse portavit
et propter scelera nostra oblatus est Christus
ALLELUIA
ITAQUE EPULEMUR (IN AZYMIS SINCERITATIS ET VERITA-
TIS)

f42v Leo fortis de tribu Iuda
hodie surrexit a mortuis
ALLELUIA
in cuius laude
celsa voce perthonate
ALLELUIA

» item «
Hec est festa precelsa
convenite omnes sacrum corpus percipere

una voce proclamantes
PASCHA (NOSTRUM . . .)
(CT III, *Tropi selecti* pp. 339—340)

If we consider the offertory and the communion tropes in these two Apt manuscripts, the situation for the same feast looks very different. First we have the same tropes in the two manuscripts with very few exceptions. We have no hexameter tropes at all but mainly biblical quotations embellished with laudatory exhortations. (Note again the invitatory form *venite adoremus.)* Further, in contrast to the introit tropes, which constitute a rather local repertory, we have here tropes that are transmitted in all regions. In other words, we cannot trace a historical pattern, such as it seemed we could among the introit tropes. What we see in Apt — that tropes of different genres have both a different character and a different type of transmission — is typical, and would be found in sources from other regions. Wherever we follow repertories, we shall notice that anytime we are tempted by an attractive generalization, we will encounter something that contradicts it. [12]

III

We shall now continue the effort to describe the trope genre by trying to place items into different kinds of systems.

Tropes are often versified — and we have more than hexameters, e. g. the quantitative Ambrosian strophe or, what is more frequent, a rythmic imitation of it. We even have quite a wonderful example of a Sapphic strophe (CT I, p.98, *Gaudeat cunctus populus per orbem . . .)* [13] There are scriptural quotations and other quotations from liturgical texts. There are tropes in a typical antiphon or responsory style. Baumstark has shown how a great number of texts beginning with *Hodie* are Latin adaptations from Byzantine sources, and exactly this style is fecund for the trope authors. [14]There are even some tropes written in the style of the orations. There is the German type of trope with a greater theological sophistication, the English type of rhetorical exuberance with a pronounced joy in using rare words, there is the typical Italian type of exhortation to praise. [15]

One could even make a classification according to length — what a difference between the short gloss-type, only one or two words inserted in the base-liturgical texts, and the long introductory songs of a more independent character. There is the established classification in terms of the music-text relation: logogene and melogene tropes. All our examples hitherto have been logogene tropes, but those where texts were underlaid to a preexisting melody must follow other laws, must be very bound by their original text. [16]

And there is yet another classification: ordinary tropes and proper tropes.

Richard Crocker has stressed the independent nature of the tropes and also the difference between tropes: proper tropes adapted to old Gregorian introits are something quite different from, say, ordinary tropes where we know nothing of the existence of the melodies before their appearance in the manuscripts provided with tropes. What Crocker calls "The troping hypothesis", has, according to his famous article of 1966, been an obstacle that has prevented people from really seeing the shifting nature of the genre called "trope".

Crocker is right when he shows how various songs called tropes can be. If we use the term "trope" for so many different things, we must of course be aware of those differences. If we call them tropes, we follow the practise of many medieval manuscripts, but far from all of them. Eva Odelman has shown in her article *Comment a-t-on appelé les tropes?* [17] that all sorts of items are called tropes in one place and by some other name elsewhere — *versus, laudes, prosa, prosula,* etc. — but that the term *tropus* is the most frequently used. The point, then, is not to think of introducing a new terminology, but rather to continue in the effort to understand what was embraced by "tropus".

First it must be stated that even the classifications already mentioned are dubious. The same trope element is sometimes used for different mass antiphons and also for different feasts. But there is much more. We can cite a few examples based on the analyses of Gunilla Björkvall in her forthcoming book on the Apt tropers.

In Apt 18 there is a prosula to the alleluia *Pascha nostrum: omnium vita mori voluisti pro cunctis salvator. O bone Iesu Christe, qui in cruce pependisti.* The same text appears as one of the elements in a Gloria trope from Winchester, Saint Evroult and Apt which has paschal themes. [18]

The well known and widely spread Easter-prosulae, *Iam redeunt gaudia* and *Christe tu vita vera* function quite clearly in Apt 18 as prosae introduced by "Alleluia", finished by "Amen" and with every strophe ending in "a". [19]

We can take our last example from the Apt manuscripts, the Gloria trope in hexameter, *Omnipotens aeterne deus, spes unica mundi/Qui caeli fabricator ades, qui conditor orbis.* Those two beginning hexameters are taken from Sedulius' *Carmen paschale I,* verses 60—61, a poem used for several different liturgical purposes. [20]

Other examples are Alleluia verses used as tropes and alleluia prosulae used as introit and offertory tropes. There are hymn strophes — and even such a very well known one as the Pentecost hymn *Iam astra Christus ascenderat* — used as introit tropes; antiphons or responsories used as proper tropes, an Agnus trope used as a proper trope or vice versa, etc. [21]

Among the most fascinating things of this kind are actually the Agnus tropes, where it is hard to say whether one really should speak about tropes at all. Among the most wide-spread are tropes which are exact quotations from the Angels' hymn, the *"Doxologia maior", Gloria in excelsis deo:*

Qui sedes ad dexteram patris, miserere nobis and *suscipe deprecationem no-stram.*

These quotations also belong to the Litany. Gunilla Iversen has argued in what we find a convincing way that in spite of their proximity to these other already established genres, we should take them as tropes when they are included together with the Agnus Dei in the manuscripts. The same can be said of the Greek version of the Agnus Dei, *O amnos,* also used as a trope.[22]

We have so far confined our attention to the linguistic component of tropes, and for the problem that concerns us here that is appropriate. For a concept of a trope genre can emerge, if at all, mainly — perhaps only — from the interaction of literary and ritual factors. But attention to the melodic aspect will produce a similar impression about the sort of tradition we are dealing with. We illustrate with a single trope complex for the introit of the mass for Pentecost, inscribed in the manuscript Benevento VI, 35 (example 3). The melody of the introductory element (40) could easily be taken for an 8th-mode antiphon (an example is given below the transcription of element 40). The style of the second element (23a) is quite different; it is the later, highly articulated and symmetrical trope-melody style that corresponds or better, responds, to the hexameter style of the verse.[23] The third element (83) presents a style typical of yet another genre, the Ambrosian hymn; it is in fact the sixth strophe of the Ascension hymn *Iam Christus astra ascenderat.*[24] And the fourth element is a direct imitation of the third.

This particular congeries of trope verses and their melodic settings is unique to this manuscript. With respect to its melodies it displays some of the same general characteristics that we have observed with respect to the linguistic aspects of tropes: composition on the model of different traditional types of ecclesiastical song, an ecclectical association of loosely connected elements, stitched together by a common function, the uniqueness of the item for a particular manuscript, and on the other hand signs of the crystalization of a style that came to be characteristic in the later stages of the practice.

If we try to come closer to a medieval conception of the tropes as a genre, it might perhaps be rewarding to go back to the oldest, most archaic manuscripts containing tropes. The two most interesting of them are without any doubt Verona 90 from Monza and München 14843 from Toul.[25] Both these manuscripts are quite important for the discussion concerning the rise of the sequences, since they also contain some of the oldest sequences. Both mss are without notation and the liturgical parts are smaller enclaves in books that contain for the most part texts of quite different sorts, e. g. texts by Isidore of Seville, various didactic texts, Carolingian rhythmical poems etc. Another interesting feature is that there seem not to be any boundaries between the different liturgical items.

Example 3

Treitler
Benevento VI 35, folio 112

40

Spi-ri-tus sanc-tus de-scendit in di- sci- pu- los

Chri- sti ho- di- e de quo gau-den-tes di- ca- mus

23 Spi- ri- tus do-mi- ni

di- sci- pu- los flam- mas in- fu- dit

pec-to- re blan-das

re- ple- vit or-bem ter-ra-rum al- le- lu- ia

83

ex om-ni-gen-te cog-ni-ti grecis la- ti-nis bar- ba- ris

cunctisque ad- mi- ran-ti- bus linguis loquuntur omni- bus

et hoc quod con- ti- net om- ni- a sci-enti- a

84

quod ex proba-tum tes-ti- bus a pos-to- lo-rum vo-ci- bus

cum sint di- versis va- ri- is lo- cu-tis o- ri- bus

ha- bet vocis alle- lu- ia alle-lu- ia alle- lu- ia.

Example 4

"In Palmis" •
Hodie fratres karissimi •
adoremus Christum filium dei
cum ramis palmarum •
DOMINE NE LONGE
Inproperium expectavit cor meum
et sustinui •
dicite filii eia •
Pater si non potest hic calix transire •
nisi bibam illum
fiad voluntas tua •
"In Pascha"
Hodie exultent iusti
resurrexit leo fortis
deo gratias dicite •
RESURREXI •
Terra tremuit et quievit
leo fortis • resurrexit dominus
deo gratias eia •
Notus est dominus in Iudea
salus aeterna •
gratias agamus deo illi eia eia •
Et factus est in pace locus eius •
IBI CONFREGIT •
Pascha nostrum ymmolatus est Christus •
ipse est enim verus agnus • eia •
VIRI GALILEI •
Ascendit deus in iubilatione •
Psallite domino
qui ascendit super caelos caelorum •
Spiritus sanctus descendit super apostolos
deo gratias dicite •
CONFIRMA HOC DEUS •
Alleluia excipias nostra studia
et gaudia manentia largiaris nobis deus • in secula •

Jn palmis· hodie frr̄ km̄· adoremus
xp̄m filium di cum ramis palmarū onendo,
Jn properium expectauit cor meum & sustinui·
dicere filii ea pr̄ si non potest hic calix tran
sire uisibibam illu fiad uoluntas tua· Jn pascha
Hodie sc̄ultem usti resur rxit leo fortis do gra
tias dicite· Resurrxit· Terra tremuit & quie
uit leofortis· resurrx̄ dn̄s do gratias ea· Nouus
ed̄r in iudea salus taine· gratias agemus do· illi
ea ea· Er factus o spacelo cus eius·
Ibi confregit· pascha nr̄m immolatus e xp̄s· ip
se est enim uerus agnus· ea· Ymigdila·
A scendit dr̄ in iubilatione· psallite dn̄o qui as
cendit sup cælos cælorum· sp̄s scm̄ descendit
sup aptos do gratias dicte· Confirma hoc ds̄·
Alt sce cipias patra studia & gaudia manentia
largiaris nobis ds̄· iuste alle··

Example 5

135

laudes ... in pascha dñi.
Oratio p(er) illa lubrica domnus canere
... dicet. Quem queras in sepulchro
celicole. Iesum nazarenu cruci
fixum oxpicole. None hic sur
rexit sicut predixerat ite nun
ciate & surrexit dicentes.

UERS. Gloria in excelsis d̄o & in terra pax hominib;
bone uoluntatis. G-H Laudat in excelsis ... terrãq;
regentē. angelicē ...us laudat & omnis homo ...

.II. T... bene dicit ouans angelica celsa potestas & mortalis
homo. ... bene dicit ouans. Benedicim... te.

.III. T... ad orat dñm cuncta caterua polorū ... tellus
pelagus laudat & orat amat. Adoram te

.IIII. Glorificant dñm ... lamina sidera c...i glorificant
rex cuncta creaturis. Glorificam te gr...s agim
tibi p...magnã gl...mcã dñe d̄ rex celestis d̄s pat
omps dñe fili unigenite ihu xpe dñe d̄s agn̄di filius
patris qui tollis peccata mundi miserere nob q...llis
peccata mundi suscipe deprecatione nrã :.

Qui sup astra sedes ad dexterã patris in altum.
rex c...i famulis tui miserere nuis. Qui sedes ad dex

134v

Gloria in excelsis deo et in terra pax hominibus bonae voluntatis
   Laudat in excelsis caelum terramque regentem
      angelicus coetus laudat et omnis homo

Laudamus te
   Te benedicit ovans angelica celsa potestas
      et mortalis homo te benedicit ovans

Benedicimus te
   Te adorant dominum cuncta caterva polorum
      te tellus pelagus laudat et orat amat

Adoramus te
   Glorificant dominum rutilantia sidera caeli
      glorificant te rex cuncta creata tuis (= tua)

Glorificamus te gratias agimus tibi . . . .
      . . . . . suscipe deprecationem nostram.
   Qui super astra sedes ad dexteram patris in altum
      rex caeli famulis tu miserere tuis

Qui sedes ad dexteram

135ᵛ

Let us first look at the proper tropes. In Mü 14843, they are on one page, fol 94 (Example 4). The two rubrics identify the feasts as Palm Sunday and Easter, but the incipits of mass antiphons refer also to Ascension and Pentecost. The rubrics do not call these texts tropes, but we can recognize them in five cases from other later manuscripts which are without any doubt tropers. Thus, the text *Hodie exultent iusti* appears in twelwe manuscripts with slight variants, *Notus est dominus* in nine and *Terra tremuit* in five.[26] Whatever these texts are in this manuscript, they are regarded as tropes in other manuscripts. Subsequently, we might take the other texts in this manuscript page as tropes, especially as their style is the same. The first one, *Hodie fratres karissimi,* for instance, is unique for this manuscript but as a type very like other tropes. Finally, the last of the texts, *Alleluia excipias nostra studia,* is a bit different in style but has the typical alleluia prosula character with all the words ending in *a,* the position of the words giving the vowels of *a e u a (largiaris nobis deus in secula).*

It is easy to see what is typical of the proper trope genre in this old manuscript. First of all, most texts are biblical. Specifically, they all belong to psalms or to other scriptural texts used in the traditional liturgy for these Easter feasts.

Secondly, there are liturgical formulas of the most current and well known type: twice the *"Hodie",* placing the text into the present, then apostrophizing of the community with *fratres, karissimi* formulas from the epistles which are often used in the Liturgy. We have the subjunctive form *adoremus* or the imperative *dicite,* belonging to the same type.

Thirdly, what is perhaps most characteristic, there are not only the short phrases giving information about the content of the feast, such as *cum ramis palmarum* or *resurrexit leo fortis* or *Spiritus sanctus descendit,* but there are even texts which are nothing else than the base liturgical texts, namely the offertory verses; but not the whole of the offertory verses, only the beginnings, followed by the most striking thing of all, *deo gratias dicite, gratias agamus deo illi eia eia.* This is exactly the type of trope found in the two Apt manuscripts, a type which thus survives even when the trope genre has developed into something else, for example the hexameter proper tropes in Apt 17. We could be tempted to define the trope genre as a liturgical text of mostly biblical content, followed by some formula containing the words *dicite eia, deo gratias.*[27]

But let us now look at the proper tropes in the Verona manuscript. (Example 5). We have two items, on fol 135 and 135v and both are provided with rubrics: *Laudes ad introitus in pascha domini,* which is astonishingly exact; it gives us not only the feast but the exact place in the mass. The text is *Quem queritis* introduced by the introduction *ora est psallite iubet domnus canere eia dicite.* On the other side of this same folio, the rubric is *Incipit laudes (sic!) ad missam in die natalis domini.* Easter comes before Christmas. This is not a "normal" liturgical manuscript.

The text is *Hodie salvator mundi de virgine nasci dignatus est. Gaudeamus omnes de Christo domino, qui natus est nobis, eia et eia,* followed by *Puer natus est nobis.* This is quite clearly an introduction to the introit of the third Christmas mass. This trope appears in 11 manuscripts from Mainz and Italy with exactly the same typical features: *Hodie,* the feast theme mentioned briefly, the exhortation to joy and the characteristic word *eia,* twice repeated. The following phrase is also well-known and wide-spread: it is the Alleluia prosula *Laus tibi Christe quia hodie cum magna luce descendisti. Dicite domino, eia, alleluia*[28].

Now, we could say that the trope genre might be defined as a kind of verse having some sort of liturgical character. The introduction function is clear. But similarly clear is the key role of the offertory texts and especially the offertory verses. If one were inclined to see the introit tropes as the very earliest of proper tropes, one would probably be mistaken. In the München manuscript we have three tropes to the offertory verse and the incipits of the offertories. Now we can come back a little to our Apt examples, where we saw that the two manuscripts, representing different ages or generations in trope-making, have nearly exactly the same offertory trope repertory. We can also see that these offertory tropes are not only enormously wide-spread, but also note that they even appear in some manuscripts that do not have other tropes. (This concerns the series *Ab increpatione et ira, Monumenta aperta sunt, Christus resurgens a morte)*[29].

Tropes as genre: — is it not then a matter first of liturgical texts used in a new context, and then newly created texts only in a later period when the hexameters invade the practice of troping?

The München manuscript also contains the hymn ascribed to Fortunatus, *Quem terra pontus ethera;* sequences, some of them very short, and the Gloria trope *Laus tua deus resonet coram te rex.*[30]

The same Gloria trope (on fol. 135v) and some of the same sequences appear in the Verona manuscript. The Verona manuscript also has a fraction antiphon and two more Gloria tropes. The first Gloria trope, *Laudat in excelsis celum terramque regentem* is entirely in elegiac distics, even with some Leonine rhymes. The text is not at all of the primitive kind that repeats already existing parts of liturgical texts, but a very conscious type of troping of the Gloria. In its style, it has a striking similarity to the so-called "versus", which are often processional songs used in Saint Gall, Reichenau etc[31]. What conclusions can we draw from all of these observations? What is typical for the trope as a genre?

First of all, there is no difference between the basic principles on which tropes and other liturgical songs and texts are made. Since the same biblical texts can be used — and in fact are used — in many different ways, also other texts can have very different functions in the liturgy. The liturgical authors act as bees, according to an image by a medieval author, flying from one flower to another and sucking the sweet honey where they can find it. We can see this procedure everywhere, for instance among the antiphons and the responsories in the editions of Hesbert, where quite a lot of versified items have been picked out from Sedulius or Fortunatus, for instance. Hymns destined for the divine office can be used in other contexts. A very interesting example of that occurred when archbishop Stephan of Liège created the first series of antiphons and responsories for the feast of the Holy Trinity. Among other things he quite simply chose the doxologies of well-known hymns which were naturally nothing other than praise to the Father and the Son and the Holy Spirit[32]. We can take such a wonderful example as the passage in some of the Italian versions of the *Exultet,* borrowed from Vergil's epic poem on agriculture, *Georgica,* in praise of bees.[33]

As this principle obtains also in the tropes, it is quite natural that we have a constant interaction between tropes and other genres, both in that the same texts appear as tropes and as other chants and also that tropes often are similar to songs of other genres.

It is not altogether incorrect to postulate some sort of evolution from a type of simple verse such as the tropes from the two very archaic manuscripts (Vro 90 and Mü 14843) to the more elaborated hexameter type in Apt 17. This is suggested especially in cases where trope writers appear to be intentionally completing a troper on an older substrate, and choose the hexameter form for their new texts. Apt 17 and the Winchester troper are clear cases[34].

We should not forget that some of the early types remained in the repertory throughout the history, and among the most interesting of those are the *Hodie* type, the *Quem quaeritis* and similar tropes. We must also bear in mind that the hexameter is not a new invention. From antiquity through the entire Middle Ages hexameters were created for all purposes, and a highpoint in the hexameter tradition is just the so-called Carolingian Renaissance. Thus, there is also an old tradition of hexameters from the beginning of troping. The Gloria trope in Verona 90 with its perfect elegiac distichs is a trope genre as old and as important as the other type of tropes.

We can summarize the subject in the following way. The oldest manuscripts make no clear distinction between tropes, sequences, fraction antiphons, hymns, etc. — There is simply some sort of liturgical bulk in a manuscript whose main contents are non-liturgical. If we look at all manuscripts containing tropes, even those with very clear rubrics, we will see that everywhere they also contain other genres, mostly sequences, or prosulas, or offertory and alleluia verses. They may be combined with tonaries, they may be graduals containing tropes and sequences etc. All this shows very well the medieval idea of the trope as a genre: the main idea is that there is one genre which is that of the mass — and which does not always have such sharp boundaries as one might think, as can be seen from the *Quem quaeritis* belonging sometimes to the mass, sometimes to matins and often being placed between the two. The Mass has some very firm and constant texts without any variants at all and some texts which change slightly and some texts which change sometimes. It seems best to see tropes as belonging to this higher order genre, the mass text, always with the mass as its center, and then with different and shifting circles of tropes, sequences, processional antiphons, verses, songs of different kinds always interfering with and influencing one another, but never isolated, never as something one ought to study apart from its context.

Notes

1. Plato, *Statesman*, 287c.
2. "El idioma analitico de John Wilkins," published in his *Obras completas,* vol. 8, *Otras inqui-siciones* (Buenos Aires, 1960) p. 142. English translation by Ruth Simms, *Other Inquisitions, 1937—52* (Austin, 1964) p. 103.
3. *Philosophical Investigations: the English Text of the Third Edition,* translated by G.E.M. Anscombe (New York: Macmillan, 1958 (66—7.)
4. For a recent general survey of scholarship treating such traditions, see Walter J. Ong, S.J., *Orality and Literacy: The Technologizing of the Word* (London and New York: Methuen, 1982).
5. The literature on the Liturgical Drama in the Middle Ages can be reached through the bibliographies: C. Stratman, *Bibliography of Medieval Drama,* New York 1972 and C. Flanigan, *the Liturgical Drama and its Tradition: A Review of Scholarship 1965—1975 (Research Opportunities in Renaissance Drama 18 (1975) pp. 81—102; 19 (1976), pp. 109—136).* Some new literature is presented in the bibliography of *Corpus Troporum III, Tropes du propre de la messe 2, Cycle de Pâques* (ed. Björkvall, Iversen, Jonsson) pp. 363—377. In the same volume, the texts of *Quem quaeritis* are edited pp. 217—223. The fundamental edition is W. Lipphardt, *Lateinische Osterfeiern und Osterspiele,* I-V Berlin 1975—76. See also S. Rankin, *The Music of the Medieval Liturgical Drama in France and in England* (Ph. Dissertation, University of Cambridge, 1—2, 1982, unpublished); *Musical and Ritual Aspects of Quem quaeritis, Liturgische Tropen,* (Münchener Beiträge zur Mediävistik und Renaissance-Forschung, hrsg G. Silagi, München 1985) pp. 181—192 and R. Jonsson, *The Liturgical Function of the Tropes, Research on Tropes,* (Kungl. Vitterhets Historie och Antikvitets Akademien, Konferenser 8, Stockholm 1983, pp. 99—123).
6. Quem quaeritis in praesepe, Corpus Troporum I, Tropes du propre de la messe I, Cycle de Noël, Stockholm 1975, p. 173—4, 261 et 279 ss; *Quem creditis super astra,* Corpus Troporum III, p. 173.
7. The best survey of definitions of the tropes is unfortunately not printed; it is an essay by Craig McKee, *The Hoping Trypothesis,* written in the University of Notre Dame, School of Theology, December 1979. It refers to R. Crocker, *The Troping Hypothesis* (Musical Quarterly, 52, 1966, pp. 183—203). See also B. Stäblein, *Tropus,* in Die Musik in Geschichte und Gegenwart.
8. The Apt trope manuscripts are treated in *Corpus Troporum V, Les deux tropaires d'Apt. Inventaire et étude analytique* par G. Björkvall, to appear in 1986. The music of the introit tropes of Apt 17 is in large measure published in *Monumenta Monodica Medii Aevi 3, Introitus-Tropen 1,* Hrsg. G. Weiss, Kassel 1970.
9. The Resurrection introit is taken from Ps. 138, 18, and 5—6, from the old version *Psalterium Romanum; Resurrexi, et adhuc tecum sum, alleluia; posuisti super me manum tuam, alleluia: mirabilis facta est scientia tua, alleluia alleluia.* The introitus verse is from the same psalm 1—2: *Domine probasti me et cognovisti me: tu cognovisti sessionem meam et resurrectionem meam.* The trope texts from the Apt manuscripts are all included in a critical edition in the *Corpus Troporum III.* Some sources of the text are also given in this edition as well as commentaries. This diplomatic version from Apt 17 is taken from the *Tropi Selecti,* pp. 322—326.

10. See new *Grove Dictionary,* articles *Psalmody* (T. Connolly) and *Invitatory* (R. Steiner).

10 bis. Cf. Gunilla Björkvall, *"Resurrexit dominus": Un trope pascal — ou deux?* (Liturgische Tropen, Hrsg G. Silagi, Münchener Beiträge zur Mediävistik und Renaissance-Forschung 36) München 1985.

11. The introit tropes for Resurrection Sunday in Apt 18 are on fol. 33v—34. See also the table in CT III, p. 257.

12. The offertory tropes for Resurrection Sunday in Apt 17 are on fol. 144—145 and those for Communion on fol. 147—148. See also tables in CT III p. 260 and 262.

13. See Peter Stotz, *Sonderformen der Sapphischen Dichtung (Medium Aevum-Philologische Studien 37)* München 1982, p. 328.

14. See A. Baumstark, *Byzantinisches in den Weinachtstexten des Römischen Antiphonarius Officii.* (Oriens Christianus II, 1936 pp. 163—187); Die Die *Hodie-Antiphonen des Römischen Breviers und der Kreis ihrer Griechischen Parallelen* (Die Kirchenmusik, X, 1909—10, pp. 153—160) and R. Jonsson, *Historia, Etudes sur la genèse des offices versifiés,* p. 39 ss, 202 et 204.

15. (Corpus Troporum = CT). An example of an Ambrosian strophe in a trope is *Ex omni gente cogniti* (CT III p. 99), of scriptural quotation *Terraemotus factus est magnus* (CT III p. 202), *Expurgate vetus fermentum* (CT III p. 100), of antiphon and responsory style *Hodie namque Christo* (CT III p. 112), *Hodie spiritus sanctus* (CT III p. 115), of oration type *Oramus te, o beate baptista Johannes* (CT II p. 87), of German type of theological treatise *Ex semine davitico* (CT I p. 321), of English rhetorical type *Lucida culmina stelligeri caeli* (CT III p. 135), and of Itaian praising style *Benigne pater* (CT IV p. 41).

16. Examples of very short tropes, "glossa type" are *Immortalis factus* (CT III p. 122), *Igneis linguis* (CT III p. 121) and *Vide pater* (CT III p. 212); of longer types are *Haec est nimis praefulgida festa* (CT III p. 108), or *Ingresso Iesu in praetorio* (CT III p. 125). Almost all the prosulae edited in CT II, *Prosules de la messe I, Tropes de l'alleluia* (ed. O Marcusson), are melogene tropes.

17. E. Odelmann, *Comment a-t-on appelé les tropes? Observations sur les rubriques des tropes des Xᵉ et XIᵉ siécles* (Cahiers de civilisation médiévale 18 (1975) 15—36).

18. *Omnium vita mori voluisti* is unique for Apt 18 (CT II, p. 120). Its first half is also a part of the Gloria trope *Laus tibi domine.* W.H. Frere, *The Winchester Troper* (H.B.S. 8, London 1894, p. 55) and A. E. Planchart, *The Repertory of Tropes at Winchester,* (Princeton 1977, II p. 274).

19. CT II, pp. 117—118; See also Chevalier, *Repertorium Hymnologicum,* nr 9363. The prose is in Apt 18, fol. 43v, without notation.

20. The Gloria trope is, in this version, unique for Apt 17, fol. 189. Carmen Paschale; CSEL X, p. 20.

21. An alleluia verse used also as a trope is *Amavit eum dominus* (CT II p. 19 and CT I, p. 58). The alleluia prosula *O redemptor omnium* (CT II, 84, II) functions also as an introit and an offertory trope (CT I p. 152), in all cases for the same feast, Epiphany. The strophe from *Iam astra ascenderat* (Walpole, *Early Latin Hymns,* Cambridge 1922, nr 116 p. 368) is *Ex omni gente cogniti,* (CT III p. 99) The antiphon *Hodie namque Christo* (Hesbert, *Corpus Antiphonalium Officii,* II, nr 3107), is an introit trope at Palm Sunday (CT III p. 112) and the responsory *Spiritus Sanctus procedens a throno* (CAO IV nr 7693) is, slightly remade, an introit trope for Pentecost, (CT III p. 116). Finally, *Aurea lux* seems to be both an Agnus trope (CT IV, p. 68 ss) and an introit trope element (CT III p. 61).

22. See CT IV, pp. 223; 229—240; 253—259 et 293. See also C. Atkinson, *O amnos tu theu: The Greek Agnus Dei in the Roman Liturgy from the Eighth to the Eleventh Century* (Kirchenmusikalisches Jahrbuch (1981) pp. 7—30).

23. For a detailed analysis of a trope in this style, see our paper "Medieval Music and Language. A Reconsideration of the Relationship," in *Studies in the History of Music, I: Music and Language* (New York: Broude Bros., 1983). P. 1—23.

24. A.S. Walpole, *Early Latin Hymns.* 368—371. Cf also note 21.

25. For Verona 90, see Crocker (ibid.), H. Spanke, *Deutsche und französische Dichtung des Mittelalters,* Stuttgart 1943, p. 33 ss); for München 14843, H. Husmann, *Tropen- und Sequenzenhandschriften* (RISM) München 1946, pp. 78—79), and W. von den Steinen, *Die Anfänge der Sequenzendichtung* (Zeitschrift für Schweizerische Kirchengeschichte 1946, p. 253—263).

26. See CT III pp. 111; 147; 203.
27. A discussion of offertory tropes of this kind takes place in J. Johnstone, *Beyond a Chant: "Tui sunt caeli" and its Tropes* (Studies in the History of Music, 1, Music and Language, New York 1983), pp. 24—37.
28. CT I p. 112; CT II p. 38.
29. Voir CT III pp. 53, 139, 68—69. Cf. John Johnstone, *The Offertory Trope: Origins, Transmissions, and Function*. Ph. D. Dissertation at the Ohio State University (unpublished) 1984.
30. Walpole, *Early Latin Hymns* p. 198; Analecta Hymnica 47, p. 282.
31. AH 47 p. 226. See also P. Stotz, *Ardua Spes Mundi. Studien zu lateinischen Gedichten aus Sankt Gallen* (Bern/Frankfurt am Main 1972).
32. R. Jonsson, *Historia,* p. 164—176.
33. See the article *Exultet* in New Grove's dictionary by Michel Huglo. See particularly *Supplementum Anianense* (J. Deshusses, Le Sacramentaire Grégorien, Spic. Friburgense 16, Fribourg Suisse 1971) nr 1022b, p. 362 and Vergilius' Georgica 152—205.
34. A. Planchart has treated this question in *The Repertory of Tropes at Winchester 1—2, Princeton 1977*. . . passim. See also G. Björkvall, CT V.

Michel Huglo

Le traité de *cantus mensurabilis* du manuscrit de Bamberg

Quand et comment les grandes cathédrales des régions de langue germanique ont-elles réceptionné l'*Ars antiqua* en usage à Notre-Dame de Paris depuis la fin du XIIᵉ siècle ? Une réponse définitive à cette question ne saurait être formulée avant que les sources théoriques et pratiques de la polyphonie parisienne aient été publiées, critiquées et datées. Dans le domaine des sources pratiques, un progrès considérable a été accompli grâce aux travaux d'Edward H. Roesner, Hans Tischler et Gordon A. Anderson — à la mémoire duquel cette étude est dédiée spécialement[1], — travaux qui prolongent ceux des « pionniers » du début du siècle, plus particulièrement Pierre Aubry et Friedrich Ludwig.

Les traités de musique mesurée copiés en Allemagne ou à destination des églises allemandes ont été par comparaison aux livres de polyphonie moins assidument étudiés, comme on peut en juger d'après l'inventaire suivant, basé en partie sur le catalogue des manuscrits de théorie musicale de la République fédérale allemande, édité par le *Répertoire international des Sources musicales*[2].

BAMBERG, Staatsbibliothek Lit.115.

Manuscrit de la fin du XIIIᵉ siècle, peut-être d'origine française, provenant du Chapitre de Bamberg.

f.1—64v : Motets polyphoniques édités en facsimilé par Pierre Aubry (1908) et transcrits par Gordon A. Anderson en 1977 (CMM. 75).

f.65—79 : Amerus, *Practica artis musicae* éditée en 1977 par Cesarino Ruini (CSM. 25)

f.79—79v (après l'explicit du traité précédent, sans titre, le traité édité ci-dessous) « Sciendum est quod in notulis . . . »

Description du ms et bibliographie dans le R I S M. B III 3 (en cours d'édition).

DARMSTADT, Hessische Hochschule- und Landesbibliothek 2663.

Manuscrit du début du XIVᵉ siècle.

f.56—69 : Johannes de Grocheo (Jean de Grouchy), traité « Quoniam quidam juvenum . . . » éd. E. Rohloff (1943) ; du même auteur, éd. facsimilé (Leipzig, 1972) de ce même manuscrit, avec en vis-à-vis le facsimilé du même traité d'après Londres, British Library Harleian 281 (voir le Compte-rendu de cette édition dans le *Bulletin condicologique de Scriptorium* 1973, n° 862.)

Description du ms et bibliographie dans le R I S M. B III 3 (en cours d'édition).

KARLSRUHE, Badische Landesbibliothek S. Peter Pm 29ᵃ

Petit manuscrit du XIVᵉ siècle contenant après le traité de Théoger de Metz (cf. GS II, p.

183—196, d'après ce manuscrit) des *Regulae super discantum* (f. 7v) éditées d'après ce manuscrit par H. Müller, Eine Abhandlung über Mensuralmusik in der Karlsruher Handschrift St. Peter Perg. 29ª, Karlsruhe, 1886, p. 1—3.

Description du ms et bibliographie dans le R I S M. B III 3 (en cours d'édition).

MÜNCHEN, Bayerische Staatsbibliothek Clm 5539.

Manuscrit de la fin du XIIIᵉ siècle ou du début du XIVᵉ, écrit à Regensburg, pour l' école cathédrale : recueil complexe de tropes, de conduits, de traités, à l'usage de la cathédrale de Regensburg. Provenance : Diessen.

f.24—27 (après un traité de plain chant, dédié à l'évêque Henri II de Ratisbonne, †1296) « Incipit Practica musicae artis mensurabilis magistri Franconis : Gaudent brevitate moderni . . . » (éd. du traité par Marie-Louise Göllner-Martinez en préparation). Suivent quelques conduits et motets.

Description du ms et bibliographie dans le R I S M. B III 3 (en cours d'édition).

MÜNCHEN, Bayerische Staatsbibliothek Clm 14523.

Recueil de quatre mss du XIᵉ au XIIIᵉ, reliés ensemble ultérieurement sous la même reliure. Provient de la bibliothèque de St. Emmeran.

f.134—159v : d'après l' inventaire de 1400 édité par El. Ineichen-Eder en 1977, cette partie constituait un libellus autrefois indépendant qui porte encore son ancienne cote LXXIIII : cf. El. INEICHEN-EDER, *Mittelalterliche Bibliothekskataloge Deutschlands*, IV 1, p.270.

Traité en vers et en prose édité par H. SOWA, *Ein anonymer glossierter Mensuraltraktat, 1279*. Kassel, 1930. La datation de ce traité a été discutée dans mon article « *De Francon de Cologne à Jacques de Liège* » : *Revue belge de musicologie* 34—35, 1980—81, p.48.

TRIER, Seminarbibliothek 44.

Manuscrit sur papier à filigranes (Briquet, n°3819), écrit en cursive du XIVe siècle, provenant de l'abbaye St. Matthias de Trèves. Il contient surtout des lettres et des modèles de lettres, puis le traité d' Annerus édité par Cesarino Ruini (C S M. 25) et enfin, au fol.136, le même traité de chant mesuré que dans le ms de Bamberg, lit.115.

Description du ms. et bibliographie dans R I S M. B III 3 (en cours d'impression).

Il faut à présent remarquer que dans le ms. d'Oxford, Bodleian Library, Bodley 77, le traité de musique d' Amerus n'est pas suivi, comme dans le lit. 115 et dans le présent manuscrit, d'un traité de chant mesuré, mais d'une liste des différents pieds de la prosodie classique avec une concordance entre ceux-ci et les ligatures de la notation modale[3]. Il est probable que, mis en face du traité d' Amerus, dont le chapitre sur la musique mesurée est vraiment trop succinct[4], les copistes ont ressenti le besoin de compléter un enseignement très sommaire par un de ces abrégés dont il subsiste en France plusieurs exemplaires[5].

Les manuscrits de Bamberg (B) et de Trèves (T) dérivent peut-être du même modèle, mais il n'est pas improbable que T, qui est si proche de B, a pu être copié sur celui-ci.

L'enseignement du traité, qui mériterait une étude approfondie, est caractérisée par plusieurs points de vocabulaire ou de doctrine. La théorie des six modes rythmiques est celle de la tradition la plus commune, formulée pour la première fois par Alexandre de Villedieu[6], en 1199 : mais ici, l'auteur distingue dans l'application le cas des motets — *motelli,* suivant la terminologie de la fin du XIIIe siècle[7] — qui étaient déchantés et le cas des *organa.* Il distingue en outre le *modus perfectus* du modus *imperfectus* comme Jean de Garlande et comme l' Anonyme IV. Même remarque pour la définition de la *figura* : mais ici, il semblerait que c'est Francon de Cologne qui est le plus proche de l'assertion de notre auteur :

BT	Francon, Cap. 4 (C S M.18, p.29)
Figura est repraesentatio soni secundum suum modum.	Figura est repraesentatio vocis in aliquo modorum ordinatae per quod patet quod figurae significare debent modos et non e converso, quemadmodum quidam posuerunt.

Observons au passage la précision de Francon et la rectification de l'opinion de ses prédécesseurs . . .

Tout compte fait, le traité copié dans BT, à la fin du XIIIe siècle, semble représenter une doctrine enseignée à Paris entre 1240 et 1260 : il n'est pas impossible que ce petit traité ait été copié après les motets de Bamberg pour initier les chanteurs à l'interprétation du *cantus mensurabilis.*

Le texte est édité ci-dessous : chaque phrase a été numérotée pour faciliter les références de l'apparatus. Enfin, un sous-titre a été ajouté au début de chaque subdivision du traité.

Notes

(1) En juin 1981, j'ai pu comparer à la Staatsbibliothek de Bamberg le célèbre recueil de motets du ms. lit. 115 à la transcription publiée quatre ans auparavant par Gordon A. Anderson dans le *Corpus mensurabilis musicae :* à mon retour de mission, j'apprenais de Ritva Jonsson l'annonce de la mort subite d'Anderson. Avec une admiration émue, je dédie à ce grand spécialiste de la monodie et de la polyphonie médiévales ce traité exhumé d'un manuscrit qu'il a si admirablement étudié.

(2) *The Theory of Music from the Carolingian Era up to 1500 :* R I S M., B III 3 : *Federal Republic of Germany* by Michel HUGLO & Christian MEYER.

(3) Facsimilé du f.139 dans l'article de Pierre BLANCHARD, « Alfred le Musicien . . . » dans *Rassegna gregoriana* VIII, 1909, c. 432 ; édition du texte par Max HAAS dans *Forum musicologicum* III (Winterthur, 1982), p.425.

(4) *Practica artis musicae,* 25 : C S M. 25 (1977), p.97 ss.

(5) Petrus Picardus, *Ars motetorum* (C S M. 15); *Ars musicae mensurabilis secundum Franconem (ibid.) ; Abbreviatio Magistri Franconis auctore Johanne dicto Baloce* (CS. I, 292—296).

(6) R. FLOTZINGER, « Zur Frage der Modalrhythmik als Antike-Rezeption », *Archiv für Musikwissenschaft* 29, 1972, p.203—208.

(7) E. ROHLOFF, *Die Quellenhandschriften zum Musiktraktat des Johannes de Grocheio,* Leipzig, 1972, p.209.

(De notulis)

[1]Sciendum est quod in notulis pro exigentia motellorum, conductorum et organorum tripliciter consideratur tempus, videlicet tempus breve quod est in brevibus notulis et illae sunt non caudatae ; [2]semibreve tempus quod est in cornutis ; [3]tempus longum quod est in caudatis et hoc est dupliciter. [4]Nam caudata potest esse duorum temporum et tunc sequitur brevis vel trium temporum, ne longa ante longam ex consideratione istorum temporum efficiuntur.

(De modis in motellis)

[5]Sex modi motellorum videlicet primus, secundus, tertius, quartus, quintus, sextus. [6]Primus vero modus consistit ex prima longa et altera brevi, juxta quem motelli ad tenorem datur talis regula quoniam eodem modo tenor se habet vel quelibet notula tenoris possidebit tria tempora. [8]Juxta secundum, qui consistit ex prima brevi et altera longa, datur talis regula quoniam sic se habet tenor vel quelibet valebit tria tempora. [9]Juxta tertium modum, qui consistit ex prima longa et duobus sequentibus brevibus, datur regula quoniam sic se habet tenor vel quelibet valebit tria tempora. [10]Juxta quartum e converso tertio. [11]Juxta quintum, qui consistit ex omnibus longis, datur talis regula quia sic est in tenore. [12]De sexto modo e converso. [13]Notandum est autem quod quatuor modis potest fieri inchoatio motellorum ad tenorem, videlicet in notula eadem aut tertia aut quinta aut octava aut in quarta et raro fit ; [14](secunda vero), sexta vero et septima penitus sunt evitandae.

(De modis in organis)

[15]Ingredientibus in organo primo videndum est quid sit modus : [16]Modus est mensuratio temporis per longas et breves. [17]Et sciendum est quod sex sunt modi quorum tres dicuntur recti, scilicet primus, secundus, sextus ; [18]et tres per ultra mensuram procedentes, scilicet tertius, quartus et quintus. [19]Et sciendum est quod omnis modus est duplex, scilicet perfectus vel imperfectus. [20]Perfectus modus est quando terminatur in tali notula in quali incipit. [21]Imperfectus modus est quando eminet in alia quam ab ea a qua incipit. [22]Item longa ante longam habet tria tempora.

---

1. notula (*pro* nota) Joh. de Garlandia II, 1 (ed. Reimer, p. 44)   5. motelli (*pro* moteti) Joh. de Garlandia II,3 (ed Reimer, p. 44)   17. rectus modus : Joh. de Garlandia I,16, ed. Reimer, p.37 ; Ano.4, ed. Reckow, p.76   18. tres ultra mensuram : Joh. de Garlandia 1,9, ed. Reimer, p.36.   20. modus perfectus . . . imperfectus : Joh. de Garlandia I,32,34, ed. Reckow p.39 ; Ano. 4, ed. Reckow p.23   22. recta longa, recta brevis *etc.* : Joh. de Garlandia I,20 ed. Reimer, p.37.

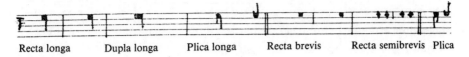

Recta longa	Dupla longa	Plica longa	Recta brevis	Recta semibrevis	Plica

(De figuris)

[23]Et debes scire quid est figura : [24]Figura est representatio soni secundum suum modum. [25]Quia omnis figura aut est simplex aut ligata aut composita. [26]Figurarum descendentium duae sunt species, id est cum proprietate et sine proprietate. [27]Recta proprietas est ut primus punctus habeat tractum descendentem a sinistra parte ; sine proprietate est ut non habeat tractum ; quando est cum proprietate, si sint duae prima dicitur esse brevis. [28]Si sint tres, duae primae erunt breves. [29]Si sint quattuor, tres primae erunt breves. [30]Si sine proprietate semper erit prima longa.

Tabula figurarum

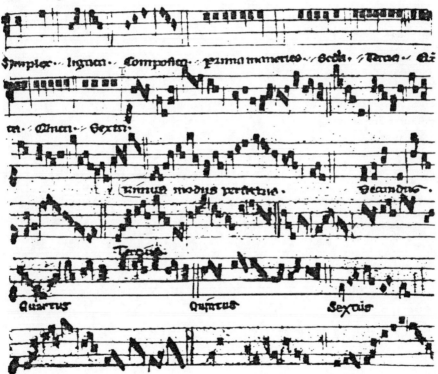

24. Figura est . . . : Joh. de Garlandia II,2, ed. Reimer,p.44   25 Figura ligata : Joh. de Garlandia II,8, ed. Reimer, p.45 ; Ano.4, ed. Reckow, p.45.

5. 2' 3' 4' 5' 6'   T 7. modo] m° B °T   8. s[ecundu]m q $_q^i$ B   2m qui T detur B   10. 4m a 3° 11. quia] quod T   12. 6° m° T   13. quod] et B   14. *ante* sexta vero *legitur* secunda vero 2a v° T) *in* BT 6a . . . 7a T.   17. sex T   VI B   19 est (*post* sciendum) *om.* T.

Wulf Arlt

„Triginta denariis" — Musik und Text in einer Motette des *Roman de Fauvel* über dem Tenor *Victimae paschali laudes.*

Die These, dass es sich bei der Motette des ausgehenden 13. und des frühen 14. Jahrhunderts in Frankreich um eine Kunst für Kenner handelt, beruht zunächst auf den beiden einzigen und daher immer wieder herangezogenen Aussagen des Musikschrifttums, in denen vom Zielpublikum der Motette die Rede ist. Die eine findet sich in Grocheos um 1300 entstandener und auf die Pariser Verhältnisse bezogenen Einordnung der musikalischen Gattungen, die andere im *Speculum musicae* des Jacobus von Lüttich aus dem dritten Jahrzehnt des 14. Jahrhunderts. Beide verbinden den Kunstcharakter dieser Gattung und die Frage seiner Vermittlung mit einem begrenzten Publikum. Johannes de Grocheo weist die Motette den „litterati" zu und jenen, „qui subtilitates artium sunt quaerentes", Jacobus beruft sich bei seiner Kritik an einigen Neuerungen des Satzes, der Aufzeichnungsweise und des Vortrags auf das Urteil eines Kreises fähiger Kantoren und kundiger Laien: auf eine „societas", „in qua congregati erant valentes cantores et layci sapientes"[1].

Worin im einzelnen die Subtilität der Kunstgestaltung liegt und worauf die Kennerschaft beruht, bleibt offen. Sicher hat beides mit dem Text und mit bestimmten Bildungsvoraussetzungen zu tun. Darauf verweisen schon das Stichwort der „litterati" und die Charakterisierung der „layci" als „sapientes"[2]. Auffallend ist weiter, dass bei beiden Autoren von der Vermittlung der besonderen Kunstgestaltung im (musikalischen) Vortrag die Rede ist, bei Jacobus unter dem speziellen Gesichtspunkt der Verständlichkeit in der Interaktion zwischen Musik und Text. So schliesst Grocheo den Vortrag der Motetten „coram vulgaribus" mit der Begründung aus, „eo quod eius subtilitatem non animadvertunt nec eius auditu delectantur", und betont Jacobus, dass sich die „moderni" um das brächten, was ihren Texten an Schönheit und Qualität eigen sei: „sic moderni, licet multa pulchra et bona in suis cantibus faciant dictamina, in modo tamen suo cantandi cum non intelligantur, perdunt ea", mit der polemischen Verdeutlichung: „Vidi in magna sapientium societate, cum cantarentur moteti, secundum modernum modum, quaesitum fuit, quali lingua tales uterentur cantores, Ebrea, Greca, vel Latina, vel qua alia, quia non intelligebatur quid dicerent."

Der Hinweis darauf, dass sich die Motette an einen begrenzten Kreis von Kennern richtet und dass sie aufgrund der subtilen Interaktion zwischen Musik und Text einen bestimmten Bildungshorizont voraussetzt, entspricht den Merkmalen der Gattung seit den ersten Kompositionen mit französischen Texten: vielschichtig im einzelnen Werk wie im Zusammenhang mit vorgegebenem Gut des geistlichen wie des weltlichen Bereichs, auf ein weites Spektrum literarischer Gattungen und Traditionen der vulgärsprachlichen wie der lateinischen Dichtung bezogen und nicht zuletzt der Liturgie, voller Anspielungen und oft raffinierter Bezüge in den Texten, in der Musik und in deren Kombination, sodass der Grundzug der Motette treffend mit dem Stichwort einer ,,intertextualité'' charakterisiert werden konnte[3]. Das erlaubte es, die Aussagen zum Zielpublikum aufs Ganze der älteren Gattungsgeschichte zu übertragen, verstellte aber zugleich den Blick dafür, dass es bis heute nur ausnahmsweise und für einzelne Kompositionen möglich war, jene Kreise näher zu beschreiben oder gar zu lokalisieren, in denen die Motetten komponiert und rezipiert wurden. So ist durchaus offen, wer in Paris Motetten schrieb — dorthin führen die älteste Überlieferung und weitere Angaben bis ins frühe 14. Jahrhundert —, wo sie dort vorgetragen wurden und bei welchen Anlässen, und wie es sich in dem weithin anonymen Repertoire mit dem Anteil anderer Städte vor allem aus dem Norden Frankreichs verhält, die in den Texten genannt werden, wie Arras, Tournai, Douai oder Cambrai. Und offen ist ebenfalls, worin die Vermittlung des besonderen Kunstcharakters im musikalischen Vortrag bestand und bestehen konnte: was von den komplexen Strukturen, von den kunstvollen Bezügen und raffinierten Anspielungen zumal dort wahrgenommen wurde, wo mehrere Texte gleichzeitig erklangen, und welche Aspekte der subtilen Interaktion zwischen Musik und Text im Hören überhaupt aufzunehmen waren.

Dass diese Fragen in der Regel nur in allgemeinster Weise diskutiert sind, hängt nicht zuletzt mit der Konzentration der musikwissenschaftlichen Arbeit an der Motette auf Editions- und Überlieferungsfragen sowie damit zusammen, dass sich die Romanistik seit den älteren Arbeiten von Gaston Raynaud und Albert Stimming nurmehr ausnahmsweise mit dieser Gattung beschäftigt hat[4]. Andererseits zeigt die Untersuchung einzelner Texte und Kompositionen, wie sich gerade dort, wo es um konkrete Aspekte jener ,,intertextualité'' geht, Anhaltspunkte zum Bildungshorizont der Produzenten und Adressaten wie zu ihrer historischen und gesellschaftlichen Einordnung, zum Kunstcharakter und zu dessen Vermittlung und nicht zuletzt zur Interaktion zwischen Musik und Text gewinnen lassen[5]. In diesem Sinn legt mein Beitrag einige Beobachtungen zu einer Komposition des frühen 14. Jahrhunderts vor, bei der mehrere Themen zusammenkommen, die Gordon Anderson beschäftigten. Es geht um eine Motette — und überdies aus einer Handschrift, deren einstimmige Teile er für die Edition vorbereitet hatte —, deren Tenor einer Sequenz entnommen ist, und im Verhältnis zwischen Musik und Text um Fragen der ,,Symbolik''[6].

*

Bei vielen der musikalischen Interpolationen im Grundbestand des 1314 abgeschlossenen *Roman de Fauvel* von Gervès de Bus, die in der Handschrift 146 des fonds français der Pariser Bibliothèque nationale erhalten sind, gab ein Stichwort des Textes den Anlass zur Ergänzung[7]. Das gilt auch für die Eintragungen auf den Seiten 21verso und 22, in deren Kontext es um die Räder der Fortuna und um die Umstände geht, die zum Wechsel des Geschicks beitragen.

Hier ist auf der linken der beiden Seiten die Aufzeichnung des Textes im oberen Viertel der dritten Spalte abgebrochen und auf der dritten Spalte der rechten Seite mit sechs weiteren Versen fortgeführt. Die Aufteilung fällt mit einer syntaktischen Zäsur am Versende zusammen und exponiert zwei Stichwörter für die musikalische Interpolation. So ist in den letzten Versen vor der Zäsur vom Auftritt der ,,Envie'' die Rede, von einem der Laster, die mit ihren Anfangsbuchstaben im Namen FAUVEL vertreten sind:

Lors vient *Envie* que s'esveille
A parler comme ce puet estre
Que tel soit si tost si grant mestre (2700—2702)[8]

Das zweite Stichwort bringt der erste Vers der Fortsetzung auf der nächsten Seite: ,,Ou peut estre que *Vérité* , . .'' (2703).

Damit beginnen die dritte und die sechste Spalte des aufgeschlagenen Buches jeweils mit einem kürzeren Textabschnitt. Die beiden dazwischen liegenden Spalten vier und fünf wurden ganz für musikalische Eintragungen ausgespart. Diese annähernd symmetrische Aufteilung ist durch die Anordnung der Kompositionen unterstrichen. In der dritten Spalte der rechten Seite steht der Anfang des umfangreichen Rügelieds *Veritas, equitas, largitas corruit,* mit dem das Stichwort der ,,Vérité'' aufgenommen ist. Dem entspricht auf der linken Seite die zweistimmige Motette *Inter amenitatis tripudia,* bei der es um den Neid geht. Das Rügelied ist erstmals aus dem zweiten Drittel des 13. Jahrhunderts überliefert[9]. Die Motette ist nach Massen der Machart sicher jünger. Doch sprechen die Überlieferung und die Aufzeichnung dafür, dass auch hier ein bestehendes Stück übernommen wurde. So handelt es sich offensichtlich um eine reduzierte Komposition, deren Text überdies auffallend eng geschrieben ist — wohl damit die Motette in dieser Spalte untergebracht werden konnte[10]. Zwischen diesen Stücken steht in den ersten beiden Spalten der Recto-Seite und mit einer unverkennbar grosszügigeren Aufteilung des Textes eine dreistimmige Motette, die nur hier überliefert ist und den Gegenstand meines Beitrags bildet.

Diese Motette bringt schon im Anfang das Stichwort des ,,Neids'', da die in der linken Spalte notierte Oberstimme mit den Worten beginnt: ,,Inflammatus invidia / demon sua malicia / primos parentes decipit'' (die Handschrift schreibt ,,inflammatis''). Den Rest der Spalte füllt der untextierte und nicht näher bezeichnete ,,Tenor''. In der mittleren Spalte der Seite steht die zweite Oberstimme, *Sicut de ligno parvulus,* die im Index der Handschrift zur Bezeichnung der Motette dient.

Aufgrund stilistischer Merkmale, des rhythmischen Verlaufs, der Klanglichkeit und vor allem der Tatsache, dass die beiden Oberstimmen in gleicher Lage ein ,,unified duet'' bilden, wies Leo Schrade die Komposition in den Umkreis der Motetten Vitrys[11]. In jedem Fall dürfte die Komposition schon aufgrund dieser Merkmale der Zeit angehören, in der ein ,,Chaillou de Pesstain'' wenige Jahre nach der Fertigstellung des Roman die Ergänzungen vornahm[12].

Die dreistimmige Komposition erscheint in der aufgeschlagenen Handschrift gleichsam eingerahmt von den beiden übernommenen Kompositionen, die jeweils erst im zweiten Viertel der Spalte beginnen. Und dass sich der Kompilator bei der Anordnung des Materials nicht nur von inhaltlichen und ästhetischen Erwägungen leiten liess, sondern damit durchaus auch Akzente hinsichtlich der Bedeutung setzte, lässt sich mehrfach beobachten. Das alles weist darauf hin, dass es sich bei dieser Motette um den zentralen Beitrag der Erweiterungen zum Stichwort des Neids handelt. Umso bemerkenswerter sind der Gesichtspunkt und die kunstvolle Anlage, mit denen in dieser Interpolation das Thema der ,,Envie'' aufgenommen und zu Gehör gebracht wird.

Nun kann es schon deswegen kein Rezept für die Interpretation einer Motette dieser Zeit geben, weil die erhaltenen Kompositionen vom ausgehenden 13. bis ins zweite Drittel des 14. Jahrhunderts eine auffallende Vielfalt der Gestaltung zeigen, mit unterschiedlichen Lösungen von Werk zu Werk. Das kann einerseits ein Aspekt jener ,,Subtilität'' sein, von der in den Texten des Musikschrifttums die Rede ist, kann andererseits aber auch auf eine Phase des Experiments in der Geschichte der Gattung verweisen, und bringt für jede Komposition die Aufgabe, den besonderen Gesichtspunkt der Gestaltung aufzusuchen. Einen Schlüssel dazu bietet bei dieser Motette ein auffallender Zusammenhang der Tenordisposition mit der Anlage, Aussage und Vertonung der Oberstimme. Ihr Text besteht aus drei Strophen, deren Verse mit jeweils anderen Reimsilben in der Folge 8 aab aab disponiert sind[13]:

Inflammatus invidia
demon sua malicia
   primos parentes decipit.
Et Abel sacrificia
5 ferens acceptabilia
   mortem de fratre recipit.

Iosephque non pepercerunt
fratres sui, vendiderunt
   hunc triginta denariis.
10 Et Ihesum crucifixerunt
Iudei et irriserunt
   maximis contumeliis.

Invidia detestari
debet que hoc operari
15   fecit et alia plura.
Precor, quod hanc imitari
non velitis, sed ornari
dei caritate pura.

Der Gang dieses Gedichts ist einfach. Er setzt mit dem Neid als Ursache des Sündenfalls ein (1—3 gemäss *Sap* 2.24: „Invidia autem diaboli mors introivit in orbem terrarum") und bringt dann in 4—6 und 7—9 die beiden häufigsten und gerade im späteren Mittelalter immer wieder herangezogenen typologischen Exempla für das Opfer Christi im alten Testament: Abel, den Kain aus Neid erschlägt, dieser Abbild der Juden und jener des guten Hirten — auf die kürzeste Formel gebracht: „Abel significat Christum, Cain populum Judaicum" (*Allegoriae in vetus testamentum* I.10), beziehungsweise mit einem Text der *Bible moralisée:* „Ce que cayn beisa son frere par traison senefie iudas qi beisa iesu crist par traison et le fist livrer a la mort de la croix" —, und dann Joseph, der wie Christus von seinen Brüdern gehasst, verfolgt und vor allem verkauft wird[14]. Dass dieser Verkauf für 30 Silbermünzen geschah und nicht für 20, wie es in der Bibel heisst (*Gen* 37.28) —, geht auf eine alte und weit verbreitete Tradition zurück, die mit Isidor und Beda ans Mittelalter vermittelt wurde und den Vergleich mit dem Verrat Christi so eng machte, wie es schon in einer Praefation des Missale von Bobbio formuliert ist: „Ille a fratribus, hic Christus Dominus a Judaeis traditur. Ille Ismaelitis triginta argenteis venditur in deserto: hic Christus Dominus triginta argenteis a Judaeis. Illum fratres vendiderunt in Egypto: hunc milites exspoliaverunt . . ."[15]. — Die Zahl Dreissig steht auch in diesem Gedicht im Übergang zum Opfer Christi, von dem der zweite Teil der Strophe handelt (10—12). Dem typologischen Aspekt der Josephsgeschichte tritt vor allem im theologischen Schrifttum ausserhalb der Genesiskommentare der tropologische zur Seite. Er ist in der dritten Strophe aufgenommen, die noch einmal mit dem Stichwort der „invidia" einsetzt, die Konsequenzen für das eigene Verhalten anspricht und im Schluss den dritten, anagogischen Aspekt der „Allegoria" aufscheinen lässt.

Der Tenor ist dem Anfang der Wipo zugeschriebenen Ostersequenz *Victimae paschali laudes* entnommen und bringt die Melodie des Eingangsversikels in einer Melodiefassung, die auch den Pariser Handschriften entspricht[16]. Dieser Anfang umfasst fünfzehn Töne. Sie sind im regelmässigen Wechsel zwischen einer Maxima und zwei Longen diponiert:

Dass dieser Abschnitt mit den beiden Kürzen endet, lässt eine abschliessende Maxima erwarten. Nun wird der Tenor dreimal durchgeführt. Damit folgt zweimal auf die beiden letzten Longen die Maxima des Anfangs. Bei einer solchen Disposition findet sich in den Motetten dieser Zeit am Schluss der Komposition in der Regel eine Dehnung der Pänultima oder ein zusätzlicher Ton. Umso auffallender ist es, dass diese Motette mit den beiden Longen endet. Damit kommt der Zusammenhang zwischen Tenordisposition und Oberstimmentext ins Spiel.

Dass die Vertonung der drei Strophen in der Oberstimme den drei Tenorfolgen entspricht — mit einer „Phasenverschiebung" bei der zweiten Durchführung —, ist nichts Besonderes. Nur wird dieser Zusammenhang hier noch dadurch unterstrichen, dass am Ende der Strophen sowie deren Hälften jeweils eine Brevis beziehungsweise eine imperfekte Longa steht, mit einer ergänzenden Longa- beziehungsweise Brevis-Pause, und dass es sich dabei, von zwei Ausnahmen abgesehen, um die einzigen Pausen in dieser Stimme handelt (dazu die Wiedergabe der Komposition nach der genannten Edition Schrades auf den folgenden Seiten 00 und 00, auf die sich im weiteren die Taktangaben beziehen). Umso auffallender ist es, dass an einer einzigen Stelle die Textdeklamation innerhalb der Strophen durch eine Longa-Pause unterbrochen ist und das zudem im Vortrag eines Verses (T. 28 in der Vertonung des achten Verses). Die Pause lenkt die Aufmerksamkeit auf die Fortsetzung. Und hier erklingt in der dreissigsten Longa beginnend das Wort „triginta"[17].

Wie planmässig die Motette auf diesen Zusammenhang hin angelegt ist, zeigt schon die Tatsache, dass es sich bei der Unterbrechung im Textvortrag um die einzige dreizeitige Longa-Pause der ganzen Komposition handelt. Die Stellung des Wortes „triginta" führt auf die Tenordisposition zurück und sie erklärt den ungewöhnlichen Schluss dieser Stimme. Denn dadurch, dass die Komposition (ohne Schlussdehnung) mit den beiden Longen endet, umfasst sie insgesamt 30 Maximae und jede ihrer Hälften 30 Longen. Dabei ist das Wort „dreissig" so gesetzt, dass es die beiden Hälften miteinander verklammert und überdies in emphatischer Weise von der ersten zur zweiten hinführt: Seine Vertonung in der Länge einer Maxima beginnt mit der letzten Longa der ersten Hälfte und endet mit der ersten der zweiten, und diese Verbindung der Teile geht mit der stärksten kadenzierenden Fortschreitung der ganzen Motette überein: mit einem Klang aus Sext und Dezime in Takt 30, dessen Strebewirkung durch die Akzidentien cis und gis unterstrichen wird, und der in Takt 31 zum perfekten Klang aus Oktave und Duodezime über der Finalis führt, mit dem Spitzenton des Stückes in der Oberstimme!

In dieser Gestaltung nimmt die Vertonung den typologischen Aspekt des Textes auf, wie er in der Oberstimme exponiert ist. Denn dort verbinden ja die dreissig Silbermünzen das Opfer im alten mit dem Opfer im neuen Testament. So wie eben in der Oberstimme bis zur 29. Longa nur vom alten Testament die Rede ist und ab der 31. nur vom neuen und seiner Konsequenz, bis zum Schluss des „ornari des caritate pura".

Der symmetrischen Anlage in zwei aufeinander bezogene Teile sowie der Gliederung in drei Strophen und mit drei Tenordurchführungen, die mit dem heilsgeschichtlichen Weg vom Sündenfall bis zur Erlösung übereingeht, lassen sich nun aber in dieser Motette noch weitere Merkmale der Gestaltung zuordnen. So ist der Text der zweiten Oberstimme in 2x10 Verse mit paarigem Reim gegliedert, die in der ersten beziehungsweise zweiten Hälfte erklingen (mit einer „Phasenverschiebung" um eine Longa, die durch die musikalische Zäsur in den Takten 30/31 bedingt ist[18]):

Sicut de ligno parvulus
generatur vermiculus,
qui post hoc idem comedit,
eo modo livor ledit
5 omnes suos possessores
et eorum bonos mores.
Invidus est totus cecus;
ignis est in eo grecus
ardens in aquis gracie
10 et in undis iusticie.

Qui accensus est hoc igne
macrescit de pinguedine
sociorum et proditor
est; iam credit esse victor,
15 quando per detractiones
deprimit fratrum honores,
et est socius demonum,
amans malum et non bonum,
quod valde dictum vicium
20 caritati contrarium.

Dieser Text handelt ausschliesslich vom Neid und von seinen Konsequenzen. Die erste Hälfte charakterisiert dieses Laster und seine vernichtende Wirkung mit einer Folge von Bildern, wobei sich aus dem Zusammenhang zwischen der Versgliederung und der Aussage eine Gruppierung in (3 + 3) + 1 + 3 Verse ergibt: Wie der Holzwurm das verzehrt, woraus er entstanden ist (1—3), so schädigt der Neid diejenigen, die von ihm besessen sind (4—6); der Neid ist blind (7); in ihm ist das „griechische Feuer", das über das Wasser der Gnade (Taufe) und über die Wellen der Gerechtigkeit hinweg brennt (und zerstört) (8—10)[19]. Der Veranschaulichung des ersten Teils folgt im zweiten eine *applicatio*. Sie konfrontiert die Aussage der anderen Stimme. Geht es dort um die Annahme des Opfers, so hier um die Konsequenzen aus dem Verharren im Neid; bis hin zu dem Schluss, der in einer seit dem 12. Jahrhundert mehrfach belegten Opposition der „caritas" das „vicium" der „invidia" gegenüberstellt, wenn es

23.(51) SICUT DE LIGNO PARVULUS.

In _ flam _ ma _ tus in _ vi _ di _ a demon su _ a ma _ li _ ci _ a primos pa _ ren _

Si _ cut de lig _ no par _ vu _ lus ge _ ne _ ra _ tur vermicu _ lus qui post hoc i _ dem

Tenor.
A

_ tes de _ ci _ pit, et A _ bel sa _ cri _ fi _ ci _ a

co _ me _ dit, e _ o mo _ do li _ vor le _ dit

fe _ rens ac _ cep _ ta _ bi _ li _ a mor _ tem de fra _ tre re _

om _ nes su _ os pos_ses _ so _ res et e_o _ rum bo _ nos mo _ res.

_ ci _ pit. Jo _ seph _ que non pe _ per _ ce _

in _ vi _ dus est to _ tus ce _ cus; ig_nis est in e _ o gre _ cus ar _ dens in a _

B

_ runt fra _ tres su _ i, ven _ di _ derunt hunc tri _ gin _

_ quis gra _ ci _ e et in un_dis iu _ sti _ ci _

_ta de _ na _ ri _ is et Ihesum cru _ ci _ fi _ xe _ runt Iu _ de _

_e. Qui ac _ cen _ sus est hoc ig _ ne ma _ crescit de pinguedi_

_i et ir _ ri _ se _ runt maxi_mis con _ tu _ me _ li _ is.

_ne so_ci_o_rum et pro _ di _ tor est; iam credit es_se vic_tor, quando per

C

In _ vi _ di _ a de _ te _ sta _ ri de _ bet que hoc o _ pe _ ra _ ri fe _ cit

de_trac_ti _ o _ nes de _ pri_mit fratrum ho_no _ res, et est so_

et a _ li _ a plu _ ra. pre _ _ cor, quod, hanc i _ mi _

_ci_us de_monum a _ mans ma _ lum et non bo _ num, quod val _ de

_ta _ ri non ve _ li _ tis sed or _ na _ ri de _ i ca_ri _ ta _ te pu _ ra.

dictum vi _ ci _ um ca _ ri _ ta _ ti contra _ ri _ _ um.

105

von dem, der vom Neid erfasst ist, heisst: „et est socius demonum, amans malum et non bonum, quod valde dictum vicium caritate contrarium"[20].

Dem Verharren im Laster entspricht in diesen Versen die gleiche sprachliche Gliederung, mit gleicher Schlussbildung: je acht Verse fallend als Paroxytonon (/.) und dann zwei steigend als Proparoxytonon (/. \). Und auch darin unterscheiden sich die drei Strophen der anderen Stimme, in denen es um den heilsgeschichtlichen Weg geht. Denn bei ihnen findet von der ersten zur dritten Strophe ein Wechsel vom Proparoxytonon zum Paroxytonon statt: die erste Strophe hat nur steigende Schlüsse (entsprechend dem Ausgang des anderen Textes); die zweite Strophe bringt bei den Versen, in denen von Joseph und Christus die Rede ist, fallende und nur beim dritten Vers („hunc triginta denariis") und beim parallelen sechsten einen steigenden Ausklang; und die dritte Strophe ist ausschliesslich fallend!

Die Disposition der Motette exponiert neben der 30 weitere Zahlen: 3 Strophen und 3 Durchführungen, mit je 10 Maximen und 15 Tönen, 2x10 Verse der mittleren Stimme und 60 Longen im Ganzen des Ablaufs. Das bringt das weite Spektrum der Zahlenallegorese ins Spiel[21]. So lassen sich auch in dieser Hinsicht zahlreiche Zusammenhänge zwischen der Gestaltung der Motette und der Aussage der Texte sehen. Die 30 kann neben dem Opfer auch auf das Jahr der Passion und der Auferstehung verweisen (nach Honorius mit einer Präfiguration im Alter Abels) und als Produkt von 5 und 6 (neben Gesetz und Gnade) auf das Heil: „triginta . . ., sub quo comparatur salus, et gratia reparatur"[22]. Die Trias wäre hier wohl vor allem als Hinweis auf die Stufung der Geschichte zu sehen: „ante legem, sub lege, sub gratia". In der 10 können der Dekalog wie das Opfer anklingen, auf das fürs Mittelalter auch die Form der römischen Zahl verweist. 15 wird gemäss den Summanden 7 und 8 vor allem als Gesetz und Gnade sowie Zeit und Ewigkeit verstanden. 60 gehört nach dem System der Fingerzahlen zur linken Hand und ist damit (nach Gregor) aufs Irdische bezogen. — Dass solche Zusammenhänge bei der Konzeption dieser Motette mitspielten ist anzunehmen, zu präzisieren sind sie freilich erst dann — und das entspricht einem Problem bei der Interpretation der Bilder und ihrer Kombination —, wenn es gelingt, den historischen Kontext einzugrenzen, in dem diese Motette entstand und für den sie bestimmt war. Dafür bieten gerade die Interpolationen des *Roman de Fauvel* aus der Verbindung von Text, Musik und Bild allenthalben Ansatzpunkte; doch handelt es sich um eine Aufgabe, die erst noch zu leisten ist.

Ein weiterer Aspekt der Gestaltung, der nicht unmittelbar in der Aufzeichnung aufscheint, liegt im Text des Tenors. Denn dass die Melodie dem unverändert und als Ganzes zitierten Eingangsversikel des *Victimae paschali laudes* entnommen ist, bindet die Texte der Oberstimme in die dreimal erklingende Aufforderung zum Lobpreis über das Opfer Christi ein: „Victimae paschali laudes immolent christiani".

Aufgrund dieser dichten Zusammenhänge zwischen Musik und Text ist kaum zu bezweifeln, dass beide aufeinander bezogen und vom gleichen Autor konzipiert wurden. Zumal diesen allgemeinen Aspekten einer ,,intertextualité'' im einzelnen eine subtile Vertonung entspricht, die eine sehr differenzierte ,,Lesung'' des Sprachtextes bietet. Sie berücksichtigt die formale Disposition, die Syntax sowie vor allem dort den Sprachfall der Deklamation, wo es um eine Hervorhebung geht, sie setzt — wie anschaulich schon die ersten Hinweise zur Vertonung der Oberstimme zeigten — klare Akzente hinsichtlich der Aussage und sie schliesst gelegentlich sogar die abbildhafte Wiedergabe einzelner Wörter ein. Die Grundlage dafür bietet ein klanglicher Abaluf, der — wie die Reduction auf Seite 104 verdeutlicht — einerseits über den gleichen Tenortönen entsprechende Klänge bringt und andererseits bei den kadenzierenden Fortschreitungen unterschiedlich gewichtet. So steht in 7/8 über dem Abstieg g-f des Tenors eine kadenzierende Fortschreitung vom Terz-Sext- zum Quint-Oktav-Klang, mit der die erste Hälfte der ersten Strophe beziehungsweise der ersten Aussage des zweiten Textes abgeschlossen wird. Bei der zweiten Durchführung hingegen findet sich an der entsprechenden Stelle eine klangliche Öffnung auf das Folgende mit dem zentralen Stichwort ,,dreissig'', da 26 und 27 (nach dem perfekten Klang von 25) mit f-a-d beziehungsweise g-h-e ein *tendere* bringen, das nur in der einen Stimme eingelöst wird: die Strebewirkung der Sext g-e in den Aussenstimmen führt in die Longa-Pause! — Eine weitere Ebene der Gestaltung liegt im rhythmischen Ablauf. Beide Ebenen greifen mit je anderem Akzent ineinander. Symptomatisch dafür ist etwa der Anfang:

So beginnt die Motette mit dem Grundmass einer Deklamation in Breven —
und gelegentlichen Semibreven —, die den Abschluss der ersten Verse mit der
3—6/5—8-Fortschreitung auf den Wechsel zum zweiten Tenorton berücksichtigt (3/4). Auch die nächsten Verse enden gleichzeitig, nur diesmal ohne *tendere*, aber dafür mit einer Longa in beiden Stimmen. Der Abschluss der dritten
Verse mit der Sinngliederung in beiden Stimmen verbindet dann die Dehnung
mit der kadenzierenden Klangfolge.

Vor dem Hintergrund dieser Spielregeln der Textvertonung wird die Gewichtung im Vortrag einzelner Wörter und Textabschnitte deutlich. Sie betrifft
in dem wiedergegebenen Anfang insbesondere die Dehnung der Deklamation
am Beginn der vierten Verse, mit der Hervorhebung des Namens ,,Abel'' und
mit dem *tendere* auf das Wort ,,sacrificia'' hin in der ersten Fortschreitung e-
gis-cis zu d-a-d (entsprechend dem ,,triginta'', aber in einer tieferen Lage). Und
wie hier der erste Name der typologischen Bezüge hervorgehoben ist, so am
Anfang der zweiten Durchführung der zweite (die Zuordnung des Textes ist
gegenüber der Edition Schrades nach der Handschrift geändert):

Das Beispiel einer subtilen Lesung, die die formalen Gegebenheiten des Verses, aber auch den Sprachfall, die Sinngliederung und die Hervorhebung einzelner Wörter berücksichtigt, bietet etwa der Schluss der Oberstimme (52—
60):

beziehungsweise in einer Reduktion auf den Deklamationsrhythmus:

Precor, quod hanc imitari / non velitis, sed ornari / dei caritate pura.

Die Deklamation unterstreicht die Wörter „precor", „hanc" und „velitis", sie bringt den Wortakzent des Sprachfalls auf die betonteren Werte — beziehungsweise bei „velitis" einen ornamentierten Hochton —, den fallenden Schluss der Verse bei unterschiedlichen Deklamationswerten immer auf die ersten beiden Werte einer Longa, und sie gliedert dem Sinn entsprechend durch den längeren Wert vor dem „sed" und die anschliessende Beschleunigung des Grundwerts der Deklamation auf den Schluss hin. — Auf diese Weise lässt sich im einzelnen allenthalben beobachten, wie die Vertonung zwischen musikalischen und textlichen Gegebenheiten kunstvoll vermittelt.

Die differenzierte Vertonung schliesst selbst die abbildende Wiedergabe einzelner Wörter ein, wie sie im 14. Jahrhundert eingehend von Heinrich Eger von Kalkar gelehrt wird[23]. So unterschreitet die Mittelstimme ein einziges Mal den Ambitus um eine Terz bis zur Finalis. Die Stelle findet sich in Takt 20, sie tritt umso mehr hervor, als die Oberstimme pausiert und der Tenor den gleichen Ton aushält, und sie fällt auf die Worte „(invidus est) *totus cecus*". Im Blick auf diese Beobachtung liegt es nahe, auch die einzige weitere Pause der Oberstimme, die nicht auf das Ende eines Abschnitts fällt, mit der Tatsache zu erklären, dass sie nach dem Wort „irriserunt" steht.

Das führt auf die Frage nach der Vermittlung der besonderen Kunstgestaltung im Vortrag zurück, von der Johannes de Grocheo und Jacobus von Lüttich sprechen. Für sie ist es von Interesse, wie viel von der musikalischen Lesung des Textes unmittelbar wahrzunehmen ist, sofern man sich bei der gleichzeitigen Deklamation auf eine der Stimmen konzentriert und zumal dann, wenn man mit dem mehrmaligen Vortrag solcher Kompositionen rechnet. So ist gerade die Hervorhebung einzelner Wörter und Textstellen deutlich auf die Wahrnehmung hin angelegt. Das gilt bei dieser Motette bezeichnenderweise am stärksten für die zentrale Aussage im Übergang von der ersten zur zweiten Hälfte, mit der Longa-Pause und der Beschleunigung der Deklamation — erst in der mittleren Stimme und dann in der Oberstimme — und für den Vortrag des Wortes „triginta" in langen Werten und in der höchsten Lage.

In diesem Zusammenhang ist es bemerkenswert, dass die Texte mehrfach mit dem Vokal der einen Stimme die Verständlichkeit im Vortrag der anderen unterstützen; so wenn in den Takten 29 und 30 unter den Wörtern „vend*i*derunt" und „tr*i*gin(ta)" die Silben „(ius)t*i-ci*(a)" erklingen oder in Takt 22 unter „(Jo)s*e*ph" das Wort „*e*(o)". Wie denn überhaupt ein ganz spezifischer Aspekt der „intertextualité" der Motetten seit dem 13. Jahrhundert in den zusätzlichen Sinnzusammenhängen liegt, die die Interaktion der Stimmen im Wechsel von der einen zur anderen mit sich bringt. Das ist hier etwa in den Takten 38—42 der Fall, wo zunächst die Oberstimme mit den Wörtern „et *irriserunt*" im oberen Klangraum liegt und nach der Pause die mittlere mit der raschen Deklamation „*iam credet esse victor, quando per detractiones (deprimit fratrum honores)*".

Andererseits bringt auch diese Motette in Musik und Text und in der Inter-

aktion beider so viele Informationen und subtile Anspielungen, dass es nahe-
liegt, den Hinweis des Grocheo auf jene, ,,qui subtilitates artium sunt quaerentes'', nicht nur auf die Vermittlung im Höreindruck zu beziehen, sondern auch
auf ein Studium der Komposition, das immer weitere Schichten erschlossen
haben dürfte. So wie es im historischen Rückblick möglich ist, aus einer Interpretation der vielschichtigen ,,intertextualité'' dieser Gattung ein Bild vom
Bildungshorizont und von der Zusammensetzung jener ,,valentes cantores et
layci sapientes'' zu gewinnen, für die die Motetten bestimmt waren.

1 — Der Text des Grocheo nach Ernst Rohloff, *Die Quellenhandschriften zum Musiktraktat des
Johannes de Grocheo,* Leipzig 1972, 144, derjenige des Jacobus bei Edmond de Coussemaker,
Scriptorum de musica medii aevi nova series 2, Paris 1867, 432a, sowie bei Roger Bragard im *Cor-
pus scriptorum de musica* III.7, Rom 1973, 95 — auf den angegebenen Seiten auch die folgenden
Zitate.

2 — Zum Stichwort der ''litterati'': Herbert Grundmann, ''Litteratus-illitteratus. Der Wandel
einer Bildungsnorm vom Altertum zum Mittelalter'', *Archiv für Kulturgeschichte* 40 (1958), 1—
65.

3 — So Pierre Bec, *La lyrique française au moyen âge (XIIe—XIIIe siècles). Contribution à une
typologie des genres poétiques médiévaux* 1, Paris 1977, 220.

4 — Die wichtigsten Arbeiten nennt das Kapitel über die Motette in der eben erwähnten Arbeit
von Pierre Bec (214—220). Nicht erreichbar waren mir die ungedruckten Arbeiten von Nico van
den Boogard, der eine für die Erforschung der Motette ausserordentlich hilfreiche Edition der Re-
fraintexte vorlegte: *Rondeaux et refrains du XIIe siècle au début du XIVe,* Paris 1969 (Bibliothèque
française et romane série D 3).

5 — An solchen Untersuchungen einzelner Motetten und bestimmter Gesichtspunkte nenne ich
folgende Arbeiten: Georg Reichert, ''Wechselbeziehungen zwischen musikalischer und textlicher
Struktur in der Motette des 13. Jahrhunderts'', *In memoriam Jacques Handschin,* Strassburg
1962, 151—169; Hans Heinrich Eggebrecht, ''Machauts Motette Nr 9'', *Archiv für Musikwissenschaft* 19/20 (1962/63) 281—293 und 25 (1968) 173—195; Reinhold Hammerstein, ''Über das
gleichzeitige Erklingen mehrerer Texte'', ib. 27 (1970), 257—286; Klaus Hofmann, *Untersuchungen zur Kompositionstechnik der Motette im 13. Jahrhundert,* Neuhausen-Stuttgart 1972
(Tübinger Beiträge zur Musikwissenschaft 2); Nico H. J. van den Boogard, ''La forme des polé-
miques et les formes poétiques: dits et motets du XIIIe siècle'', *Die Auseinandersetzungen an der
Pariser Universität im XIII. Jahrhundert,* ed. A. Zimmermann, Berlin/New York 1976, 220—239
(Miscellanea medievalia 10).

6 — Die meisten der Arbeiten Gordon Andersons zur Motette des 13. und frühen 14. Jahrhunderts verzeichnet der Artikel über ihn in *The New Grove Dictionary of Music and Musicians* 1
(1980), 399/400. Sie sind um einen posthum erschienenen Aufsatz zu ergänzen: ''New Sources of
Mediaeval Music'', *Musicology* 7 (1982), 1—26. Seine eingehenden Quellenstudien zur Überlieferung der Sequenz, die nicht mehr in eine Publikation eingingen, gaben uns den Anlass zu mehreren
Begegnungen mit ebenso hilfreichen wie anregenden Gesprächen. Von einer für das *Corpus mensurabilis musicae* vorbereiteten Ausgabe der einstimmigen Stücke des *Roman de Fauvel,* deren
Fahnenabzüge bei einem Basler Seminar Gordon Andersons vorlagen, berichtete er schon in ''The
Rhythm of the Monophonic Conductus in the Florence Manuscript as Indicated in Parallel Sources
in Mensural Notation'', *Journal of the American Musicological Society* 31 (1978), 480—489,
insbesondere 482 n. Schliesslich galt eine seiner letzten Arbeiten dem Thema ''Texts and Music in
13th-Century Sacred Song'', *Miscellanea Musicologica* 10 (1979), 1—27.

7 — Viele dieser Zusammenhänge verzeichnet Emilie Dahnk, *L'Hérésie de Fauvel,* Diss. Leipzig 1935 (auch als Leipziger Romanistische Studien II. Literaturwissenschaftliche Reihe 4). Eine Faksimile-Ausgabe dieser Handschrift mit einer eingehenden Einleitung von Edward Roesner, der im Juli 1984 in Certaldo am Kongress *L'Europa e la Musica del Trecento* zusammenfassend über seine Beobachtungen zu "The Making of the *Roman de Fauvel"* berichtete, ist im Druck.

8 — Die Verzählung nach der Ausgabe von Arthur Långfors, *Le Roman de Fauvel par Gervais de Bus,* Paris 1914—19, 97.

9 — Dazu die Angaben in der Ausgabe von Dahnk sowie bei Gordon Anderson, *Notre-Dame and Related Conductus: Opera Omnia VI: 1 Pt Conductus Transmitted in Fascicule X of the Florence Manuscript,* Brooklyn 1977, 147.

10 — Eine Edition der Motette bei Leo Schrade, *Polyphonic Music of the Fourteenth Century* 1, Monaco 1956, 42, dazu die Angaben im Kommentarband, 83/84. — Auf weitere Beispiele für Reduktionen und Kürzungen von Kompositionen aus Platzgründen wies Edward Roesner in "The Making of the *Roman de Fauvel"* hin.

11 — "Philippe de Vitry: Some New Discoveries", *De Scientia Musicae Studia atque Orationes,* ed. E. Lichtenhahn, Bern/Stuttgart 1967, 300.

12 — Dass dieser Chaillou nicht mit Raoul Chaillou identisch sein kann, der für die Jahre 1313—22 als "bailli" nachgewiesen ist, betonte Edward Roesner in "The Making of the *Roman de Fauvel".*

13 — Dazu die Ausgaben von Dahnk (106/107) und Schrade (*Polyphonic Music,* 43/44), der die Emendationsvorschläge der Textausgabe übernimmt. Die Handschrift weicht an folgenden Stellen von der Lesung Schrades ab: 1 —Inflammatis; 3 — primo; 6 — ferre (statt fratre); 16 — invitari.

14 — Das Zitat der *Allegoriae* nach PL 175, 340c, und des Texts der *Bible moralisée* nach der von Alexandre de Laborde edierten Handschrift (fol 2verso): *La Bible moralisée illustrée* 1, Paris 1911. — Zum typologischen Zusammenhang: die einschlägigen Artikel im *Lexikon der christlichen Ikonographie,* ed. Engelbert Kirschbaum, insbesondere 1, Rom 1968, 5—10 ("Abel und Kain") sowie 2, Rom 1970, 423—435 ("Joseph von Ägypten") mit weiterführenden Angaben zu Quellen und Literatur, sowie zur Josephsgeschichte die eingehende Untersuchung von Manfred Derpmann, *Die Josephgeschichte. Auffassung und Darstellung im Mittelalter,* Ratingen etc. 1974 (Beihefte zum "Mittellateinischen Jahrbuch" 13).

15 — nach Henri Leclerq, "Joseph", *Dictionnaire d'Archéologie Chrétienne et de Liturgie* 7, Paris 1927, 2654/2655.

16 — So etwa in der Handschrift latin 1112 der Bibliothèque Nationale.

17 — Auf diesen Ansatzpunkt für eine Interpretation der Motette führte eine Arbeitsgemeinschaft des Wintersemesters 1983/84 an der Universität Basel zum Roman, der ich für diesen Beitrag Anregungen verdanke, insbesondere der Herren Jorge Espinach und Lorenz Welker. Dass wir uns damals auch die Herkunft des Tenors "entdeckten", erwies sich im Nachhinein als unnötig, da er schon im Inventar der Handschrift von Gilbert Reaney genannt ist: *Manuscripts of Polyphonic Music (c1320—1400),* Duisburg etc 1969 (Répertoire International des Sources Musicales B. iv. 2).

18 — Im Wortlaut folge ich wieder der Ausgabe Schrades, der einen Emendationsvorschlag der Ausgabe von Dahnk übernimmt. Er betrifft folgende Stelle: 12 — pingridine. Ausserdem macht Dahnk auf den Reim der Verse 15/16 aufmerksam: "detractiones"/"honores".

19 — Die Geschichte dieser Bilder lässt sich im einzelnen von den Kirchenvätern über Kommentare und Predigten des Mittelalters bis zu den verschiedensten allegorischen Texten und Darstellungen des späten Mittelalters dokumentieren; doch war es mir bisher nicht möglich, ihre Verbindung und Gewichtung in einem historischen Kontext der Zeit um 1300 zu verankern.

20 — Zur Opposition caritas-invidia im *Hortus Deliciarum* der Herrad von Landsberg: Adolf Katzenellenbogen, *Allegories of the Virtues and Vices in Mediaeval Art from Early Christian Times to the Thirteenth Century,* London 1939, und generell der Artikel "Tugenden und Laster" von Michael W. Evans, *Lexikon der christlichen Ikonographie* 4, Rom etc. 1972, Sp 380—90.

21 — Dazu die grundlegende Darstellung von Heinz Meyer, *Die Zahlenallegorese im Mittelalter. Methode und Gebrauch,* München 1975 (Münstersche Mittelalter-Schriften 25), der ich bei allen nicht weiter nachgewiesenen Angaben folge. Zur Technik jetzt auch Hanne Lange, *Les données mathématiques des traités du XIIᵉ siècle sur la symbolique des nombres,* Kopenhagen 1979 (Université de Copenhague. Cahiers de l'Institut du moyen-âge grec et latin 32) und zur Interpretation literarischer Texte die Überlegungen von Ernst Hellgardt, *Zum Problem symbolbestimmter und formalästhetischer Zahlenkomposition in mittelalterlicher Literatur,* München 1973 (Münchner Texte und Untersuchungen zur deutschen Literatur des Mittelalters 45).

22 — So die *Analetica numerorum et rerum in theographyam,* secunda clausula 3.21, ed. H. Lange, Kopenhagen 1981, 153 (Cahiers de l'Institut . . . 40).

23 — Zu diesem Zusammenhang zwischen der Chorallehre und der mehrstimmigen Musik die Überlegungen bei Wulf Arlt, "Musik und Text im Liedsatz franko-flämischer Italienfahrer der ersten Hälfte des 15. Jahrhunderts", *Schweizer Jahrbuch für Musikwissenschaft* 1 (1981), 64—67, sowie die Untersuchungen von Fritz Reckow: "Rectitudo — pulchritudo — enormitas. Spätmittelalterliche Erwägungen zum Verhältnis von materia und cantus", *Musik und Text in der Mehrstimmigkeit des 14. und 15. Jahrhunderts. Vorträge des Gastsymposiums in der Herzog August Bibliothek Wolfenbüttel 8. bis 12. September 1980,* Kassel etc. 1984, 1—36 (Göttinger Musikwissenschaftliche Arbeiten 10).

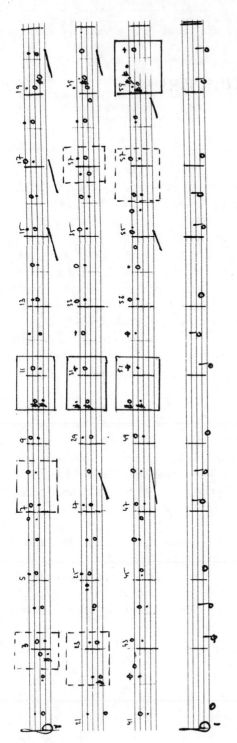

• = *Inflammatus invidia*
° = *Sicut de ligno parvulus*

Zur leichteren Orientierung sind in der Regel nur die Klänge auf dem Anfang einer Longa aufgenommen, mit Ausnahmen dort, wo es um die Interpretation bestimmter Klangverbindungen geht. — Die kadenzierenden Fortschreitungen der Oberstimmen sind mit einer Abstufung nach ihrem unterschiedlichen Gewicht eingerahmt. Schräge Striche verweisen auf kadenzierende Fortschreitungen nur in einer der Oberstimmen.

CORPUS TROPORUM:

CORPUS TROPORUM 1. Tropes du propre de la messe 1. Cycle de Noël. Ed. R. Jonsson et al. Studia Latina Stockholmiensia 21, Stockholm 1975.

CORPUS TROPORUM 2. Prosules de la messe 1. Tropes de l'alleluia. Ed. O. Marcusson. Studia Latina Stockholmiensia 22, Stockholm 1976.

CORPUS TROPORUM 3. Tropes du propre de la messe 2. Cycle de Pâques. Edition critique des textes. Ed. G. Björkvall, G. Iversen, R. Jonsson. Studia Latina Stockholmiensia 25. Stockholm 1982.

CORPUS TROPORUM 4. Tropes de l'Agnus Dei. Ed. critique suivie d'une étude analytique par G. Iversen, Studia Latina Stockholmiensia 26, Stockholm 1980.

CORPUS TROPORUM, Concordances de tous les mots des éditions, avec les contextes, des volumes 1—4. Non imprimées, à consulter au bureau du Corpus Troporum de Stockholm.

CORPUS TROPORUM 5. Les deux tropaires d'Apt mss. 17 et 18. Inventaire, analyse et édition des textes uniques par G. Björkvall. Studia Latina Stockholmiensia 32. Stockholm 1986. (in print)

CORPUS TROPORUM 6. Prosules de la messe 2. Les prosules limousines de Wolfenbüttel. Ed. critique des prosules d'alleluia du ms. Wolfenbüttel, Herzog August Bibliothek Cod. Guelf. 79 Gud. lat., par Eva Odelman. Studia Latina Stockholmiensia 31, Stockholm 1986. (in print)

Research on Tropes. Kungl. Vitterhets Historie och Antikvitets Akademien. Conferences 8. Ed. Gunilla Iversen, Stockholm 1986.

Liturgische Tropen. Referate zweier Colloquien des Corpus Troporum in München (1983) und Canterbury (1984). Münchener Beiträge zur Mediävistik und Renaissance-Forschung, hrsg. Gabriel Silagi. Bei der Arbeo-Gesellschaft München 1985.